DIVINE WEALTH

A Financial Awakening for Women Ready to Rise

FRANCESCA REA, CFP

Divine Wealth

Print ISBN: 978-1-66641-559-9
eBook ISBN: 978-1-66641-561-2
Edited by: Anna Filippone
Cover Design: Media Vandals
Formatted by: Jennifer Traynor

To my reason why:
Keeler and Aidan
Keep shining your bright lights
Be the best that you can be
Let no one take that away from you!

Contents

Author's Note vii

Chapter 1: A Whisper of Courage: Zoe 1

Chapter 2: Between the Waves: Zoe 9

Chapter 3: The Doorway to Prosperity: Lilly 19

Chapter 4: Beyond the Silent Judgment: Zoe 27

Chapter 5: Money is a Tool: Sofia 33

Chapter 6: Shift Your Money Mindset: Barb 45

Chapter 7: Your Wealthy Self-Image: Mikayla 53

Chapter 8: Worthy By Design: Zoe 67

Chapter 9: Vision of Prosperity: Lori 79

Chapter 10: Harnessing Your Queen Energy: Lilly 91

Chapter 11: Lifetime Habits of Prosperity: Roxanne 97

Chapter 12: Rising Up: Zoe 111

Chapter 13: Mindful Money Solution: Julie 117

Chapter 14: Building a Wealth Blueprint: Dorothy 131

Chapter 15: Are You Covered? Zoe 145

Chapter 16: The Celebration: Lilly 155

Chapter 17: Final Climb: Zoe 177

Reflection Exercise: The Courage Inventory 191

Action Step: You're Worthy of Receiving 193

Mini Challenge: Your Prosperous Self Postcard 195

The Mirror of Admiration 197

Exercise: Define Your Financial Purpose 199

Journal Prompt: What Do I Really Believe? 201

Rewrite Your Self-Image Script 203

Create Your Own Luxury Shopping Experience 205

Create Your Own Vision Board 207

Discovering Your Queen Energy 209

Mini Exercise: Create Your Domino Habitat 211

Daily Gratitude Ritual 213

Create Your Mindful Money Solution 215

Reflection Exercise: Wealth Blueprint 217

Journal Prompt: Protecting What You Have 219

Create Your "Queen's Toast" 221

Reflection: Letting Go 223

Acknowledgments 225

About the Author 229

Author's Note

There comes a moment in every woman's life when she looks around and realizes: Is this how my story was meant to be?

For me, that moment came the day I discovered my husband was having an affair. Looking back, I can see that something greater than me was guiding that unraveling, showing me this was not my true path. My inner voice had been whispering to me for years, but I didn't listen. I kept pushing it down, ignoring it, hoping things would somehow get better. I worked harder. I did more. I tried to control everything, believing these traits were the keys to success.

I had everything I thought I wanted—a marriage, two beautiful children, a home in Toronto, a cottage by the lake, and a career I loved. From the outside, it looked perfectly composed. But inside, I was dying a slow death. Everything I thought was secure suddenly crumbled, and I was exhausted from holding it all together.

I truly believe that day became the second birth of me. She had been there all along, the real me, but she was too afraid to speak, too scared to shine.

In the years that followed, I began to unravel everything I thought I knew about money, success, and self-image. As a wealth advisor, I had spent decades helping others build wealth, yet I was terrified to look at my own bank account. I wasn't just rebuilding my finances after divorce; I was rebuilding *myself.*

I began to realize that money is far more than dollars and cents. It's a tool. It's energy. It's a reflection of how we see ourselves. Slowly, I saw that money had never been the enemy—my beliefs around it were. The fear, guilt, and scarcity I carried weren't mine; they were inherited stories passed down through generations.

When I started to examine my life like a scientist with curiosity instead of shame, I began to rewrite those stories. And when I did, something miraculous happened: my outer world shifted in response. I stopped believing that earning money had to be hard, that safety came from struggle, or that worth was earned through exhaustion. Instead, I turned inward and began the real work of healing my relationship with myself and with money.

When I focused on my self-image and daily habits, when I slowed down and got clear on my vision, and saw my future self, that is when everything changed. My relationship with my children deepened. I created space for joy again. I became more present, which allowed me to tune into my intuition, that quiet voice I'd ignored for so long, and life began to respond. People, opportunities, and money started showing up with ease. Within six months, I had doubled my income, not by working harder or adding more chaos, but by working smarter, softer, and in flow. I paid off the debt that had weighed me down for years. I stopped hustling for worthiness and started receiving from a place of self-trust.

Then a familiar idea resurfaced—the one I'd whispered thirty years earlier: *Write that book you've dreamed of.* This time, the message was clear: *Now you have your story.*

My healing journey led me through a process that blended the practical and the spiritual, the mind and the heart. This shifted my belief that prosperity isn't about what you earn or accumulate, but about what you embody, which is not widely accepted in the traditional financial world, but I'm here to change that.

Those realizations became the foundation of *Divine Wealth.*

I walked these steps myself before ever teaching them to others. Each one turned my fear into trust, chaos into clarity, and striving into receiving. This is not just a book about money or personal finance. It's a book about becoming whole.

Divine Wealth is the story of eight women who come together on a life-changing retreat and uncover the truth about money, power and the stories we've been told. Each carries her own version of fear, shame, avoidance, and longing. Through their journeys, you may see reflections of your own—the over-giver, the caretaker, the perfectionist, the dreamer, or the woman frozen by indecision and fear. Through heartbreak, healing and hilarious moments of honesty, they transform their relationship with wealth and themselves.

Maybe you've felt the ache of not enough, or the quiet guilt of wanting more. Wherever you are, know this: there is no shame in starting here. Every chapter is an invitation to return home to yourself.

While each woman's story is unique, the thread that weaves them together is the same truth that changed my life: Money is a mirror. It reflects our boundaries, our worth, our values, and our fears. When you shift your relationship with money, you don't just change your finances—you change your frequency.

Divine Wealth unfolds in two layers. On the surface, I take you to Bali—a journey much like the one I took after my divorce, where Zoe, the main character, attends a prosperity retreat. Her mentor, Lilly, guides each woman through her own awakening. Beneath the story lies the roadmap: an eight-step process to creating prosperity on purpose. Each step leads the characters through transformation, and my hope is that, while reading, it will ignite your own.

Awareness without action fades quickly. Too often, we begin the process of change only to slip back into old habits. That's why I have created a section at the back of the book devoted to integration with journal prompts, reflections, and simple exercises to help you bring these lessons to life. Think of it as a personal retreat in written form.

My ultimate goal for *Divine Wealth* is to show you that balance exists—between strategy and surrender, between the masculine and feminine energies of money and that you can stand tall, as the queen that you are, in the center of it all, regardless of your circumstances.

My hope is that this book becomes more than something you read. I want it to spark a lifelong passion for your own financial prosperity. Let it be a companion, a quiet voice reminding you to slow down, breathe, and trust that everything you need is already within you. You don't have to have it all figured out. You just have to be willing to begin.

We cannot do this alone. Women rise when we rise together. When we support one another to be bold, brave, and visible, we heal generations of silence around money.

Divine Wealth is my love letter to that freedom.

This is the book your future self will thank you for.

Chapter 1

A Whisper of Courage

Zoe

My chest felt tight, each breath shallow as if my lungs couldn't quite fill. Standing in the waiting area, I held my passport and boarding pass tightly in one hand and my carry-on handle in the other. I shifted my weight from my left foot to my right and back again, my stomach a swirling storm of anxiety, fear, and guilt around leaving my children behind. My mind raced with questions and doubts, the heaviness of the past year pressing down on my shoulders.

Five years of deceit. Five years of shared meals, conversations about the kids, and building a bright future together with a newly purchased cottage were all undermined by whispered plans and stolen glances. My stomach twisted as I thought of the countless hours I had spent with my friend next door, blissfully unaware of how much time she had spent alone with my husband.

How blind had I been? The betrayal still burned even though my marriage was officially over the moment I signed the divorce papers a few weeks ago. And now I'm boarding a plane to Bali. Shaking my head, all I could think was how I didn't even know myself anymore. The old me would have sat at home and cried alone. This version? I jumped at the chance to go on a wealth retreat with my favorite financial guru, whom I followed on Instagram.

I took a deep breath. It was time to figure out who I want to be. I'm tired of overspending on shoes, pinot grigio, and things that the kids don't need but make me feel, in the moment, like I'm the best mom in the world. No more numbing my insecurities with retail therapy and expensive dinners because I feel like a total failure in life.

My thoughts were interrupted when my section for the plane was called over the speaker. After checking my boarding pass and passport, I walked through the bridge onto the airplane. I shuffled down the aisle, clutching my paperwork and trying to ignore the ache that had settled permanently in my chest. My leggings showed signs of wear, and the oversized sweater I wore felt like a shield against the world—soft, shapeless, and utterly unremarkable. I felt invisible.

Passing through the first-class section, my gaze drifted to a woman lounging in one of the plush, wide seats. Her head was turned away as she laughed at something the person beside her said. A cream silk blouse matching her linen pants radiated effortless wealth and style. Her legs were crossed with precision, and her manicured fingers, adorned with a massive emerald-cut diamond, cradled a glass of champagne that sparkled under the soft cabin lights. The faint scent of something expensive—perfume, hair products, a life I'd never know—seemed to float around her like an aura.

Resentment churned in my chest, sharp and bitter. She was everything I wasn't: Put together. Luxurious. Confident.

Everything about her screamed a life that felt so far removed from mine it might as well have been fiction. I glanced down at my scuffed sneakers and felt my face flush. She probably didn't even own sneakers like these. Would there ever be an occasion when she would wear a baggy sweater like mine? She clearly had married the right man, considering the size of her ring. He provided her with the lifestyle and confidence I never got from mine.

As I continued down the aisle, I felt it wasn't fair that she had the life I wanted handed to her on a silver platter. I've worked so hard and yet can't imagine achieving that kind of lifestyle. And she was the embodiment of everything I'd lost: the sense of control, the self-worth, the marriage that had once made me believe I was part of something special. Now I had nothing. I desperately wanted to be her.

I moved on to the economy section and slipped into my cramped seat, gripping my boarding pass so tightly it had crumpled in my hand. Anger simmered just beneath the surface, hot and insistent. Despite my best effort to hold it all in, tears slipped down my cheeks, uninvited and unstoppable. I swiped at them furiously, but they kept coming, betraying me. I turned my face toward the window, pretending to look outside, though all I could see was the reflection of my own miserable expression. The seat beside me remained empty, and I prayed it would stay that way.

I took a deep breath, trying to calm myself and stop the tears from flowing.

Then I recognized it: A familiar song playing softly in the background.

"Lovely Day" by Bill Withers.

My breath caught in my throat. Mark and I had danced to this song on our wedding day, swaying together as though the world had disappeared and we were the only two people who existed. It was the best night of my life... I was marrying my soulmate and starting the life of my dreams.

But it all came crashing down with one message.

3

It had been an ordinary night, a casual dinner with Mark's mom and sister. Chloe and Brooks were running around the house, laughing and trying to pull me into their game of tag, and the smell of grilled chicken wafted in from the backyard. I'd gone to change the Spotify playlist—something upbeat to keep the energy going—using Mark's phone, which was connected to the speakers. After more than ten years together, we knew each other's passwords and often used each other's phones to Google and play music. When I unlocked it, a message popped up on WhatsApp.

Happy 5th Anniversary, Mark.

At first, I thought it was a mistake. My breath caught as my thumb hovered over the notification. My brain screamed at me to put the phone down, but my body acted on instinct. I opened the chat and started to read dozens of messages.

Clutching the phone, my legs carried me outside before I knew what I was doing. Mark stood at the grill, beer in hand, the epitome of suburban calm. The world tilted as I screamed, "What the fuck is this?" I held the phone up, shaking with rage.

Mark's eyes widened, and he reached for the phone, but I darted past him, scrolling furiously through the messages. The conversation stretched on and on. Years of messages, photos, plans, jokes, declarations of love. Pam. Our neighbor, Pam. The one whose husband, Greg, had waved at me that morning while mowing the lawn. The Pam who helped me after my difficult birth with Brooks. The Pam with whom I drank wine as we complained about our husbands.

My vision blurred with tears as I pieced together the timeline. I turned toward the neighbors' house, my voice rising. "Pam! Get the fuck out here, Pam! You want to celebrate your anniversary with my husband, then get the fuck out here! Get out here and get your man, Pam! Greg! Greg, you may want to come, too. You need to hear this!" I screamed at their screened patio door.

Mark's mother and sister had come outside, their faces masked in shock. Chloe and Brooks were crying now, clinging to their grandmother, terrified. The scene was chaos, but all I could see was betrayal.

I turned back to Mark and spat, "Pack your shit and get out." My voice was low and shaking, but there was steel in it. "Get the fuck out of here, NOW!"

I shuddered from the memory, and the tears flowed again, hot and unchecked. I wiped at them angrily, grabbing my book out of my bag for distraction so I could get my emotions under control. The words swam before my eyes: *Eat, Pray, Love.* I'd bought it impulsively at the airport gift shop, hoping for a lifeline, a guide out of the wreckage of my life.

A woman sat down beside me, taking the unoccupied seat. While I quickly wiped the tears off my face, she asked, "Are you okay? Are you afraid to fly?"

I shook my head from side to side, unable to speak. I wasn't at all afraid to fly, but I wasn't sure if I was brave enough to be on this plane after our wedding song played. I tried to convince myself that this was just a freak coincidence. Maybe it was a sign from the Universe that I was leaving Mark behind, as well as my attachment to this song.

"Interesting choice," she added. I turned to find the woman watching me with concern. She had to be in her eighties. She was tiny, yet anything but frail. Lines etched her face, but even with her concern, her pale blue eyes twinkled, framed by a halo of silver curls.

"Excuse me?" I asked, unsure if I had heard her correctly.

"The book," she said, gesturing toward the copy of *Eat, Pray, Love* I had placed on my lap. "Everyone turns to it when their life falls apart. It's practically a rite of passage."

I lowered my head, heat rising to my cheeks. "I guess I'm just another cliché," I muttered, my voice tighter than I intended.

Her smile softened, her eyes warm and disarming. "Oh, darling, I didn't mean it as an insult. It's a fantastic book. It made me want to go to Bali and, finally, here I am."

That caught my attention. "You're flying to Bali because of this?" I asked, holding up the book.

"Well, to be truthful, I never read the book. I loved the movie, though. For the last few years, I thought I was too old to do anything Julia Roberts did, but here I am," she said, leaning back in her seat with a graceful ease.

Her words hung in the air between us, a bridge between two strangers.

"I'm Nora," she said, smiling.

"Zoe," I replied, feeling awkward looking her directly in the eye.

"Nice to meet you, Zoe. You don't look too excited about going to Bali. Looks like you're going through one of the tougher seasons of life."

I blinked, the lump in my throat returning. "What makes you say that?"

She studied me for a moment, her gaze steady, but kind. "Maybe the tears in your eyes," she said simply. "And the way you're holding on to that book as if it's a lifeline. You're ready for something new. Time to go after it."

A tear slipped down my cheek before I could stop it. I wiped it away quickly, embarrassed, but Nora didn't look away. If anything, her expression softened further, her sympathetic presence being just what I needed.

"It's okay to feel all the emotions of what you're going through," she said gently. "But don't let it stop you from moving forward."

I glanced down at the book in my lap, my fingers tracing the edges of its cover. "You're not wrong," I admitted softly. "My marriage just ended. I'm trying to figure out what's next."

Nora nodded knowingly. "Ah, the dreaded what's next. It's a terrifying question, isn't it? But also the most liberating one."

My lips twitched into a small smile. "I'll let you know when I feel liberated."

I exhaled slowly and glanced out the window, the tarmac blurring as the plane began to taxi. I closed my eyes and leaned my head back against the seat, letting the hum of the engines drown out the noise in my mind. For now, I would let myself disappear into the pages of someone else's story. Mine was too painful to face.

***

To reflect on this chapter, please go to page 191.

Chapter 2

Between the Waves

Zoe

As I stepped off the plane, the Bali heat enveloped me like a thick, sticky wave, fragrant with the scent of tropical flowers. Shielding my eyes from the brightness, I marveled at the unexpectedly flat expanse of land after leaving the mountains of Sicily. The jungle landscape displayed every hue of green, and I watched palm trees gracefully swaying in the gentle breeze in the midst of it. The scene felt tranquil, and I sighed, closing my eyes as the warmth of the sun kissed my skin.

After collecting my bags, I strolled through the bustling terminal, the chatter of travelers blending with the hum of rolling suitcases. On my left, I caught sight of the woman from first class elegantly sliding into a sleek black luxury sedan, guided by a chauffeur in a black suit and crisp white shirt who was holding her door. He bowed his head, closed the door without a sound, took the driver's seat, and drove off. For me, hiring a local driver to take me to the hotel seemed luxurious when I booked it, but watching her get into that high-end car with a professional chauffeur hinted at a whole new realm of extravagance.

To my right, a line of men, all similarly dressed in white t-shirts and black pants, stood holding name placards. Scanning the names, I spotted my driver at the far end. A smile spread across his face as our eyes connected. He jumped forward to greet me.

"Welcome to Bali, Ms. Zoe," he said warmly in clear English with a soft Indonesian accent. "I'm Gusti and I'm happy to be your driver." He grabbed my bags with ease. "Let's get you going on your trip," he continued as we walked toward the parking lot. No curbside pickup for me.

As we drove, all the different sights overwhelmed me. The contrast between old and new was jarring—ancient statues and shrines nestled between tropical flowers, right next to a McDonald's. It made me pause. Was this harmony or contradiction? I wasn't sure. From a North American viewpoint, the traffic was complete madness. Cars and motorcycles, ignoring traffic rules, whizzed by on all sides of us. Surprisingly, no one seemed angry or frustrated. Without any evidence of rules, everyone shared the road with an unspoken courtesy that was completely foreign to my driving experience at home.

As we weaved through the traffic, a knot tightened in my stomach. It suddenly dawned on me that I didn't know this man. I was halfway around the world, alone in a car with a stranger and had no idea if we were going the right way. Was this brave or foolish?

Gusti must have sensed my unease. He gently started sharing some of the history of Bali. He pointed out Garuda Wisnu Kencana—one of the tallest statues in Indonesia—that was inspired by a story from Hindu mythology about the search for the elixir of life. Feeling more comfortable, I asked about the black-and-white checkered cloth I saw wrapped around trees and monuments along the side of the road. He explained that *poleng* signifies the harmony and coexistence of opposing forces like good and evil, light and dark, and positive or negative. His voice calmed me, and I smiled, thinking balance was exactly what I needed.

He soon quieted, his concentration focused on navigating the incredible melee of traffic that had increased as we came closer to the city center. I sat back, and my mind drifted to the events that led up to this trip. The chaotic week before I left for Sicily, my parents replayed in my mind—signing divorce papers, transferring the house into my name, endless packing, the hustle of work, and cherishing every moment with my children. Then, I spent a week in the Italian landscape, celebrating my parents' fiftieth wedding anniversary while feeling like a complete failure for not making my own marriage last.

Overwhelming emotions from that time flooded back, bringing with them a wave of nostalgia and sorrow. The weight of being away from Chloe and Brooks for so long settled heavily on my chest, leaving me with an indescribable feeling of emptiness and yearning. It was a whirlwind of emotions that I hadn't had a chance to fully process.

And then sheer panic hit me. How was I going to pay for all this? I had nearly maxed out my credit card for the trip and knew that reality would hit hard when I got home. I had impulsively booked this trip for me, a reward for getting out of that marriage, without much thought of my finances.

In this unfamiliar place, seated in an SUV with a friendly stranger, my eyes were brimming with tears as a combination of sadness, fear, and the beauty of Bali overwhelmed me. Despite the difficulty, I knew I had to do this for myself. I needed to find myself in the fragments of my new life. It was my only hope.

By the time we pulled up to the hotel, I had calmed myself and committed to enjoying every moment. I looked out the car window and was stunned by the blend of modern luxury and traditional Balinese design. The architecture, the soft golden light, the sheer scale of it all... it felt like stepping into a dream. From the moment I signed up for the retreat, I told myself this was the start of a new life. But standing here now, taking it all in, nothing could have prepared me for how real that promise suddenly felt.

This wasn't just a beautiful hotel. This was confirmation. A living, breathing symbol that maybe—just maybe—I was stepping into something far bigger than anything I'd ever let myself believe I deserved.

Gusti grabbed my bags, and I followed him into the grand foyer. He led me to the front desk and explained who I was to the concierge. He then turned to me. "We are still going to the Tanah Lot temple tomorrow, correct?"

"Yes, absolutely," I said. A blog post I'd read about Indonesia mentioned that it was a must-visit. A strong feeling prompted me to go, so I'd scheduled the car service in advance.

"I will be here promptly at nine a.m. and have everything prepared for our adventure." Folding his hands, he bowed his head, then turned and walked away.

After checking in at the front desk, a staff member guided me down a quiet corridor into a cozy meeting room. It was serene and elegant, with soft music playing in the background. A woman in her twenties greeted me with a warm, open smile.

"Hi. I'm Reagan, from Lilly's team. Welcome to Bali and to the *Rise Into Prosperity Retreat*. Let's get you registered. Your name?"

"Zoe Miller."

"Ah, here you are," she said as her finger glided down a printout of names before stopping at mine. "Here is your name tag, and in this bag, you'll find all the information you need for the retreat." She handed me a lanyard—a necklace strung with carved wooden beads bearing a small plastic cover that held my name tag. She also gave me a beautiful, boxy handwoven rattan bag with a braided trim and handle. The interwoven black and gold pattern reminded me of the *poleng* cloth I saw adorning trees and statues on our way to the hotel. The coarse material was a stark contrast to the glittering gold tissue paper peeking out.

"Do you have any plans before the retreat starts?" Reagen asked.

"I'll be visiting Tanah Lot tomorrow. My driver, Gusti, has arranged it. My Sunday schedule is still up in the air, though. What would you recommend?"

"I could give you some ideas, but they wouldn't be as good as what your driver might suggest. If he is taking you to Tanah Lot, then I'm almost positive he can plan another epic adventure for you on Sunday," Reagan said, beaming. "If you need anything else, though, please feel free to ask."

"Thank you," I said. "I appreciate it."

As I turned to walk away, I saw her.

Lilly Ainsworth.

My breath caught in my throat, and I froze mid-motion. She had just walked into the room like she owned it: Designer sunglasses perched effortlessly on her head, a cream silk shirt, slim linen trousers, and a silk scarf that shimmered with every step. I did a double-take as I realized it was her—the woman from first class. The one who'd slipped into that luxury sedan at the airport while I stood there clutching my carry-on, exhausted.

I hadn't seen her face on the plane because her head was turned as I passed by, but I now recognized her instantly. I had spent many moments during the flight quietly resenting her poise, her ease, her elegance. She looked like a woman who was born into a world of luxury, while I had been fighting tooth and nail to keep my head above water.

But I knew who she really was. Lilly Ainsworth. *The* Lilly Ainsworth. Her Instagram feed had been the final push that made me book this trip. Post after post, she radiated confidence, financial freedom, and a kind of purpose that stirred something deep inside of me. She was the spark for the vision of who I secretly wished I could become.

And now she was walking straight toward me.

"Hi, I'm Lilly," she said, her voice warm and confident, her smile genuine. Holding out her hand, she continued, "Welcome to Bali and the *Rise Into Prosperity Retreat*."

I stared. Words? Where were my words?

"Um—hi. I'm—uh—Zoe." I cringed at how awkward I sounded. Of course, I would trip over my name. I gave her a limp handshake and then thrust my arm down by my side, trying not to think about how disheveled I looked.

But Lilly didn't even blink. Her smile held steady. "It's so nice to meet you, Zoe. I hope you're as excited about this retreat as I am. Starting Monday, your life is going to change." Her eyes sparkled like she meant every word.

I nodded, gripping my tote bag a little tighter. "Super excited," I said, though that didn't begin to cover what I was feeling. Overwhelmed. Starstruck. Maybe a little nauseous. And deeply, deeply unprepared.

She turned to the woman who had handed me my materials. "Just checking in, Reagan. Is everything good?"

"All set," Reagan replied. "Zoe's one of the first to arrive. The rest will be flying in over the next couple of days."

"Perfect." Lilly gave a nod, then turned back to me. "Before we officially begin, and if you are interested, there is an amazing hike along the river, which will take you to a little spot to meditate. It's breathtaking—life-changing, even." She winked. "See you in a few days."

And just like that, she floated out of the room, that same effortless grace trailing behind her.

I let out a long exhale I hadn't realized I'd been holding. My hands were trembling as I gripped the handle of the rattan bag. This wasn't just a photo of Bali pinned on my vision board collecting dust for years; I was living it. I had secretly dreamed of a life like Lilly Ainsworth's. It was all coming together as if it had been planned like this all along.

I turned toward the hallway and saw the same hotel staff member who'd guided me in, patiently waiting.

"Are you ready to see your room now?" she asked with a gentle smile.

I nodded, still a little shell-shocked, and followed her to the elevator. We rose to the third floor, then walked down a quiet hallway until she stopped in front of room 333.

"Here you are," she said, unlocking the door.

Room 333, I thought. *Now that's a great sign.*

I stepped inside, inhaling deeply, and smelled fresh jasmine. The room was unreal: Floor-to-ceiling silk drapes. A grand canopy bed with crisp white linens. Two towel swans curled together at the foot of the bed like they were in love.

I walked slowly around the space, running my fingers along the polished wood of the dresser. My heart whispered a question I'd been too afraid to ask: *Do I really deserve this?*

I slid open the French doors and stepped onto the terrace. There, tucked into lush greenery, was a private outdoor shower. It looked like a secret garden. I smiled for the first time in days.

For the first time in years, I felt... worthy.

Worthy of beauty.
Worthy of indulgence.
Worthy of putting myself first.

***

The next morning, Gusti picked me up early. He had given me clear instructions on what I had to wear and brought me a kebaya that covered my shoulders and arms, a sarong to wrap around like a skirt, and a selendang sash to wrap around my waist, which he explained symbolized a desire to limit negative thoughts in one's mind.

"Now," he said with a proud smile, "we go to Tanah Lot."

Tanah Lot temple took my breath away. Built on a rock slowly being swallowed by the sea, it rose like a dream out of the crashing waves. The sand was black, a deep contrast to the temple, glowing a gorgeous yellow in the morning sun. Priests sat silently on the rocks, watching.

As Gusti instructed, I approached with my offering, a basket filled with fruit, flowers, and money—a gesture of gratitude for life's blessings meant to honor the gods and maintain balance between the spiritual and earthly worlds. One of the priests gently blessed me with holy water, placing a thumbprint of rice on my forehead.

It stuck there, warm and sacred. I walked slowly up a steep set of stairs, the scent of incense growing stronger with every step.

I stood alone inside the temple, admiring the rich colors—reds, golds, purples—softened by time but still vibrant. As the clamor of the crowd outside softened, I realized that the other tourists didn't have the proper clothing to wear inside the temple, so they were refused entry. Thanks to Gusti, I was welcomed.

I laid down the offering on top of the shrine in the middle of the temple. Then, I was guided to a mat. I sat down, lit a stick of incense, and closed my eyes.

The high priest began chanting and ringing a bell. And behind it all were the waves, continuous and hypnotic. Their roar and crash, steady and ancient, filled every cell of my body. I had never heard anything like it.

It's going to be okay, Zoe, my heart whispered. My tears flowed freely, washing over me with a profound sense of peace and acceptance. Though in a strange place, I had an overwhelming sense of belonging.

Afterwards, Gusti and I walked to a small restaurant perched along the shore. We sat quietly, toasting to a beautiful day while watching the sun begin its descent. The sky turned golden, the waves kissed the shore, and I felt something I hadn't in a very long time: Home.

As I sat in the golden hour light, still wearing the ceremonial garb, I closed my eyes and turned my face to the sun.

Gusti looked at me and said softly, "You look like Lakshmi, the goddess of beauty and good fortune."

And for once, I had hope that this was true.

***

Ready to take action on receiving more in your life?
Proceed to page 193.

Chapter 3

The Doorway to Prosperity

Lilly

Bali hums with a kind of magic that gets into your skin before you even realize it.

This morning, the faintest hint of sunrise touched the eastern sky as I slipped on a turquoise blue camisole and navy blue linen palazzo pants. With a steaming cup of coffee in hand, I stand barefoot on the warm teak deck, gazing at the crystal-clear water of my private infinity pool, feeling the sun's warmth on my skin. I breathe deeply, trying to calm myself. I didn't expect to feel this nervous.

I'm seventy years old, for God's sake. I've spoken on stages to thousands. My clients have included Fortune 500 CEOs and professional athletes. I've sold over a million copies of my book, *Sacred Prosperity: How to Align, Receive, and Rise*. And yet here I am, fidgeting with the diamond clasp on my bracelet, my palms damp, and my heart beating a little faster than normal, like this was my first time speaking.

They think I have it all.

They're right, in a way. I have a villa in Tuscany, a penthouse in New York, a husband who adores me, and a granddaughter who draws pictures of "Grandma Lilly the Magic Lady." I wear Prada like it's The Gap, and I fly business class not because I need to, but because I have earned the luxury of not arriving cramped and exhausted.

This is my very first small group retreat, and it sold out in a matter of days. Eight women from around the world are here in Bali to spend a transformative week with me. They don't know each other yet, but they've all seen my face, read my book, and watched my TED Talk. They will walk in expecting Lilly Ainsworth: The global prosperity coach with the vintage Ferragamo clutch, designer clothes, and a life with a high-vibe husband in a picture-perfect world. They don't know what it took to get here.

And maybe... maybe that's the problem.

Because how do you teach about real transformation if you don't start with the truth?

A bright blue butterfly with delicate wings lands gently on the teak table beside me. Delicate. Free. I used to envy creatures that seemed so free and untroubled, their lives a stark contrast to mine. Now I teach women how to become them. But this week will only work if I go first.

Can I really tell them the truth?

I've wrestled with this all morning. The story I have never told, a secret I have carried for years. The one that cracked everything open. Part of me, the cautious and protective part, wants to keep it hidden. After all, your image is everything. But another part— the wiser part, the softer part—knows that to truly connect, I'll need to take the first step toward vulnerability.

So, I take one last look in the mirror. I adjust my hair, now a soft golden blond, with just enough volume to say: *Yes, I've arrived.* And I walk out the door.

The meeting room looks even better now that it is set up the way I envisioned it to be. It's a private, round retreat space nestled at the edge of the jungle, mere steps from the ocean. A wraparound balcony, bordered by a wooden railing in a diamond lattice pattern, circles the entire structure. The sliding Balinese doors—beautifully and intricately carved from jackfruit wood—are wide open, letting in the warm ocean breeze. In the distance, the waves create a rhythm that calms your nervous system before you even realize it needs calming.

The teak hardwood floors, polished to a mirror sheen, reflect the morning light. Above, the roof soars into a high, peaked dome, open at the top to let the air flow, with a wide ceiling fan turning lazily, creating a gentle whoosh.

My team has set up eight small round tables, one for each woman, creating a wide circle along the outer edge of the room. Each table displays a gold-inked name card, a luxurious journal embossed with *Rise Into Prosperity,* and a serene white lotus flower floating in a simple stone bowl. A smaller circle of soft orange yoga mats and meditation cushions fill the center of the room, ready for the meditation portion of the retreat. The room glows with a comforting warmth and a sense of joyful expectation, validating that I am right where I am supposed to be.

At the back of the room, fresh mango slices, coconut yogurt, croissants, and a steaming carafe of rich, Balinese coffee sit on a long mahogany table.

I walk to the front of the room and stand beside a simple carved wooden chair.

I don't sit.

I breathe.

Then I hear them: The first footsteps.

One by one, the women arrive. They don't speak to each other. Instead, they politely nod and exchange smiles before quietly retreating to their assigned tables. Following the last woman's arrival, I prolong the silence, creating anticipation and suspense.

Then I begin.

"Hello and Welcome."

All eight heads are now turned toward me.

"I'm Lilly."

I let out a long breath. "Wow, I didn't think I would be this nervous. This is the first time I'm putting on *Rise Into Prosperity* as a small-group retreat. This is something I've wanted to do for a long time, but haven't had the space in my calendar to make it happen. Today, that changes."

A few women clapped awkwardly.

"Ladies, it's ok to make some noise; this is worth the applause."

That raised the level of enthusiasm.

"The intention of this retreat is not only for all of you to rise to your desired level of prosperity, but also to provide you with the money and mindset tools to stay there. And, of course, to have some fun along the way."

That made them smile.

"We are going to go deep, ladies. Deeper than your comfort zone, because that is where transformation lies. At the end of this retreat, some of you are not going to recognize yourselves... in a good way," I said, beaming at them. "As you can see on the agenda, it says we will be starting with yoga. And we will do that a bit later. But to start off, I wanted to set the stage for the week by sharing something with you I have never shared before. I have struggled because there is so much shame around this. It has a lot to do with trusting who you are speaking with and not having this on TMZ by morning. I am trusting you now with one of the worst times in my life, in hopes of you trusting me for the rest of the week."

The room went quiet.

I gesture lightly to myself. "You know, the woman on the book cover, the keynote speaker, the jet-setter."

I see nods. They've seen the Instagram feed. The Forbes list. And I can feel it now—the part of them that's comparing. The voice inside each of them saying: *She's nothing like me.*

"But what you might not know—what no one really knows—is who I was before I became her."

I nod my head and rock back and forth on my heels, trying to build confidence to share my story.

"This is a story I've never told on a stage. Not in a book. Not even to my children. This is the shame I have carried for decades, and it is time to bring it to light so it can heal—and this is the place to do it. I want you to play full out while you are here this week. And I need to be open to doing the same."

That catches them off guard.

"I was twenty-nine, a single mother of three children under the age of six. Their father was long gone, and I was working two jobs—daycare assistant and part-time waitress—trying to make rent and keep the lights on."

A few of the women leaned forward.

"I was exhausted. I was angry and frustrated. One afternoon, I went to Walmart. I had twenty-three dollars left in my bank account, and I needed milk, formula, and diapers. But I also needed socks, diaper cream, and granola bars. I don't even know what came over me. I was so desperate to provide for my kids that I stuffed the extra items into the stroller under the blanket. I convinced myself that this was what I needed to do to survive. And I promised myself I'd come back and pay for them next week."

A beat of silence.

"I thought I was invisible."

A breeze blows in from the open doors.

"I wasn't."

I let the moment hang.

"The security guard stopped me at the door and asked to look under the blanket. I remember the heat rising in my body, the kind that makes your ears ring and your face flush. He asked if I had anything else in the stroller. I lied. He leaned down and pulled back the blanket, saw the hidden items, and then called the police."

With a heavy sigh, I lower my head. For a moment, I wasn't sure if I could continue; doubt, cold and heavy, settled in my chest. With a nervous throat-clearing, I look back at the expectant faces of the participants.

"They didn't arrest me. But they threatened to. They said they would call child services. That I could lose all three of my children. I begged. I wept. I told them I didn't know what else to do. I was tired. I was ashamed. And I have never been so afraid in my life."

Tears prick my eyes, but I blink them away.

"And then... something inside me snapped again. But not in fear this time. In resolve. I packed my children, Ashley, Naomi and Austin, in my crappy car—the one that I prayed would start every time I turned the ignition. I remember driving home in silence. And then when I got home, got the kids a snack, and found a moment to myself, I said to the Universe: "I am never living like this again. You show me a way out, and I'll walk it, no matter what.""

My throat tightens, but I don't look away.

"That night I wrote a vision. Not because I believed it yet, but because I couldn't survive without one. I wrote: *I am a wealthy woman. I help others become wealthy, too. My children are proud of me. I live a life of elegance, ease, and joy.*"

I smile.

"Ladies, that was forty years ago. And everything I wrote came true."

I see the women shift uncomfortably in their seats, unsure of how to react.

"You look at the life I have now and think I must have had it easy. Maybe I married well. Or I slept my way to success. I've heard the whispers."

A few women glance at each other, caught.

"My husband is a beautiful man. But I had already made my first million before I met him. I built this life from scratch with purpose and belief in myself, leaving behind the fear and shame I felt that day in Walmart."

I let the information sink in before continuing. "I didn't come here to impress you," I say, my voice steady. "I came here to remind you that your past does not define your future. Your mistakes do not determine your worth. And your story—no matter how messy—is the foundation of your magic."

The sun shifts. A stream of light pours into the room like a sign from the Universe.

"I used the exact tools I'll be teaching you this week to go from poverty to a millionaire. I used them when I was tired, when I was scared, and when no one believed in me. And I kept going. Because I knew I was meant for more."

I look around the room. Every woman is listening to every word.

"I tell you this story, not for pity. But for integrity. And so you'll believe me when I say this: I know where you are. Each of you came here because something in your life is not working. You've hit a ceiling or you've hit rock bottom. Or maybe you've hit both. And I know how to get you where you want to go because you, too, are meant for more."

I take a step forward.

"And we start... with truth." I pause and I look at each of them one by one. "I've told you my story. Are you ready to share yours?"

***

Ready to take on a mini challenge? Please go to page 195.

Chapter 4

Beyond the Silent Judgment

Zoe

Beads of sweat trickled down my forehead, a mixture of anxiety and the stifling heat. I looked around, the disorienting, quiet, and unfamiliar surroundings jolting me back to reality as if from a dream. I was in Bali. *What?* The memories came rushing back in a tidal wave of emotion—a mixture of happiness, sadness, and blame—all the feelings that led me to this place.

Anticipation of the week ahead brought a sickening wave of apprehension, an icy dread that left my stomach in a tight, queasy twist. The thought of sitting among strangers and imagining Lilly's silent judgment when she finds out who I really am was too much for me.

I stood beneath the ceiling fan, its blades a blur, feeling the slightly cooler air that was still thick with humidity. Overheated and sweaty, I knew I needed to cool down before I could even attempt to get dressed.

I glanced in the mirror, pleased to see a healthy golden glow on my skin, a testament to the sun's warmth over the last few weeks. Since makeup isn't really my thing, I enjoyed the freedom of this natural look. I applied a pale pink lipstick, the faintest hint of blush, and a light brown eyeliner, creating a natural and soft look. The ceiling fan had dried my short bob, leaving it slightly tousled and smelling faintly of the summer air. Between work and kids, a stylish haircut was a low priority; my schedule demanded a quick and efficient, no-frills approach.

I inhaled deeply, wishing the air would somehow infuse me with the bravery I lacked. Another wave of nausea washed over me as I thought about walking into that room, a place where I felt utterly out of place. But with the miles I traveled, the money I spent, and the voice that told me to do it, I needed to believe I was where I was meant to be. With a deep breath to steady my nerves, I got dressed quickly and walked out the door.

As I entered the meeting room, I realized I was only the second participant to arrive. Lilly stood at the front of the room, looking impeccable in blue, speaking quietly with Keeley, one of her assistants, her words barely audible. The other participant was a stunning woman who looked as if she'd stepped off the cover of a magazine. Her coiled hair framed a face with flawless, earth-toned skin. A gold-stitched pattern accented the crisp navy linen dress she wore. She sat poised and serene at her table. Her appearance suggested she was attending a relaxed lunch date, a stark contrast to the firewalk I was expecting. I leaned over to read the small, embossed name tag on the polished wooden table: Mikayla Fenty. Even the spelling of her name was elevated.

A nervous sweat slicked my palms as I sat at the round table marked "Zoe Miller." The other women drifted in, one by one, each wearing a beautiful outfit that matched the heat and vibe of Bali. One wore a hand-painted silk caftan, the colors vibrant and rich, while another woman's sundress billowed behind her like a wedding train. It seemed that everyone's hair and makeup were impeccably done, each looking polished and professional.

I tugged at the hem of my cotton dress—a yellow thing I had thought was sweet and tropical when I packed it, that now felt juvenile and wilted. The back stuck slightly to my skin from the combination of Bali heat and a nervous sweat I couldn't seem to shake. Everyone else looked airbrushed. I looked... melted.

I looked up at the last participant to arrive. Her short, wavy, sandy brown hair, touched with gray at the temples, framed a face etched with the wisdom of a woman in her late fifties. That sandy brown hair was a wild mess, seemingly untouched by a brush this morning. Clad in green cargo shorts, a beige linen shirt, and Birkenstocks, she was a stark contrast to the crowd, even more so than I was. I wanted to know her story.

No one spoke. Each person quietly grabbed what they needed from the refreshment table and found their seat. They each focused on arranging their journals and pens, making sure their coffee and water were within easy reach. It was the only sign of nervousness I could see.

With a small sip of my coffee, I avoided eye contact, my gaze fixed on the retreat schedule, the smooth paper a stark contrast to the anxiety churning in my gut. Truthfully, I didn't understand half of it. *Breathwork activation. Nidra yoga. Chakras.* The words were so foreign, it felt like I was reading another language.

I watched Lilly at the front of the room, her blonde hair catching the light as she spoke. The heat seemed to have no effect on her. In a silk sleeveless shirt and linen pants, she exuded an aura of calm, radiating power. My stomach twisted. I knew women like her, women who carried themselves with a quiet confidence that commanded attention.

Women like her didn't sit in the food court after school, trying to budget what fast food her kids could eat so she could stretch grocery money for a few more days. Women like her didn't wake up at three a.m., terrified they'd made a mistake in the divorce settlement. Women like her didn't let tears fall, muffling the quiet sobs in the shower, to hide the sound from the kids.

A shift in the air preceded her words, and I instinctively sat straighter as she spoke. I expected a recital of her accomplishments, each word building a ladder of her endless triumphs, deepening my envy. Instead, she shared a story so compelling it left me breathless.

She'd been a single mom. With three children. Working two jobs.

Wait? What?

I quickly scanned the room to see if anyone else reacted in surprise, like me. But most of the women were listening intently, their expressions soft and thoughtful. I felt my heart thud in my chest. This woman, a vision of polished elegance and effortless grace, was once like me? If this is true, then what does this mean for me?

The recalibration of my idea of her sent my head reeling; then, she spoke again, and my breath hitched. She, Lilly Ainsworth, the epitome of success and perfection, had shoplifted.

I stared at her. Not in judgment. In complete and utter disbelief. She was there, in front of us, the sting of humiliation still clear in her voice as she recounted the Walmart incident. In desperation, she hid granola bars under a blanket, an act that nearly landed her in jail and cost her custody of her children. Something cracked inside of me. I blinked furiously and pressed my hand to my cheek, wiping away a tear.

The raw honesty in her story cut through the wall of emotional isolation I had built around myself since my divorce, a wall that had kept everyone at arm's length. I thought I had to be perfect, polished, and successful to belong here. But maybe, just maybe, broken belonged too.

And then, her voice tight with anger, she addressed the persistent, degrading rumors she had "slept her way to the top."

Heat rose in my cheeks, and the shame felt like a physical weight pressing down on me. I was one of the people who believed it. It was the first thing that came to mind when I saw her on the plane. But it wasn't only about her. This was my standard response, a ready-made excuse to explain away the huge accomplishments of so many successful married women. My failure felt less painful, their success less annoying, if I could simply chalk it up to their fortunate choice of husbands. It was easier than admitting that she had the belief, tenacity, and vision that I didn't.

Then she said, "I didn't come here to impress you. I came here to remind you that your past does not define your future."

Her statement hit me like a physical blow, the words echoing in my mind—a sharp, stabbing reminder of the self-doubt I have carried my entire life. And then the betrayal by my husband and best friend left me feeling so broken... I couldn't imagine ever being seen as whole or valuable again. Until today.

I swallowed hard. My throat burned. I grabbed my pen like a lifeline and flipped to the first page of the *Rise Into Prosperity* journal sitting in front of me. In shaky handwriting, I wrote:

My past does not define my future!

This is the first day of the new me.

A single tear smudged the dark ink as it hit the page, leaving a blurry trail. Looking at my hands, the ones that had wiped away my children's tears, signed the divorce papers, and held a glass of wine far too often late at night, I realized that they had witnessed it all. And now they are writing a future brimming with possibilities I hadn't dared to dream of.

Then Lilly said, "I've told you my story. Are you ready to share yours?"

The blood drained from my face. Tell my story? I couldn't even say my ex-husband's name out loud without my blood boiling. No one outside of my family knew the truth about what happened with Pam—how humiliating it was, and how it still haunts me when I close my eyes at night.

How could I possibly tell that story here? To strangers.

My head screamed a resounding "no"—a powerful voice of reason. But somewhere beneath the fear, beneath the burning shame that flushed my cheeks, there was a flicker of hope that someday I would be ready.

Maybe I didn't have to fake confidence or show up with a perfect story, perfect clothes, or perfect anything. Maybe all I had to do was stay in this room and be open. A deep breath calmed me, and then, with a sigh of relief, I decided that was good enough for now.

Lilly's eyes landed on me, just for a second. Our gaze locked. Her expression didn't say, *"Are you ready?"* It said, *"It's going to be okay."*

I gave the slightest nod, my head barely moving, a subtle acknowledgement. The affirmation, a quiet, external declaration, wasn't for her; it was for me. My hand trembled as I reached for my pen, adding the sentence: *I'm not ready to tell it yet. But I'm ready to find the truth.*

And this time, the tears that slipped down my cheeks didn't feel like failure.

They felt like freedom.

***

For a self-reflection, proceed to page 197.

Chapter 5

Money is a Tool

Sofia

So, I never imagined I would be a 30-year-old woman living in my mother's basement. Yet, here I am. Or, more like it, there I was, less than forty-eight hours ago, staring at my phone screen with its stupid crack, toggling between my declining bank balance and the Pinterest board titled *Mi Vida Nueva*. My dream life pictured on that board was free from everything I despised in my life—the anxieties of credit card debt, the sleepless nights, and the living at home again.

All my friends had settled into their lives, owning houses and condos, getting promotions, marrying, and starting families—some were even expecting their second kid. Meanwhile, I was painfully single, ghosting collection calls, and still shopping online like I was a millionaire. And I hated myself for it.

Then, my mom generously paid for this retreat. "I want you to go find yourself," she said, her voice low and urgent, as she put the plane ticket in my hand. "I want you to have a better life than I did, Sofia. You are too vibrant, too full of light, to be confined to a basement."

Tears welled in my eyes when she spoke those words, in part for the gift itself, but also because I felt the sting of an undeniable truth. I was absolutely and totally hiding from all my failures in that basement, even though it was a constant reminder that I wasn't where I was supposed to be.

If my mother hadn't paid for this, I probably would have ditched today's retreat session, choosing a long, lazy morning instead. What can a woman like Lilly Ainsworth, who would never understand my life, possibly do to help me? The thought of disappointing my mother, with her hopeful face and the quiet pride in her eyes, kept me from staying in bed.

I made sure that my makeup was impeccable. It's something I pride myself on and a testament to my dedication to the endless YouTube tutorials I've watched, but I underestimated the time it would take, so twisting my damp hair into a messy bun was the only practical solution for my curly mop. I smoothed the soft fabric of my new jumpsuit, pleased with how it hugged my body and felt so light against my skin. Because I'm petite, the right fit makes all the difference in how an outfit looks. Then I rushed out the door.

Most of the participants were already seated by the time I got there. I scanned the room, seeing many of the participants in beautiful outfits and noting the confident vibe they owned, like they knew something I didn't. A nervous smile touched my lips as I mumbled a hello. I quickly grabbed a croissant and a cup of coffee before taking my seat at the table that bore my name.

I kicked off my sandals and felt the cool, polished teak floors beneath me. I was trying not to sweat through my brand-new jumpsuit that—to be honest—I purchased to play the part of good-enough-to-be-here. It wasn't just the heat causing all of this perspiration. I was also freaking out about people finding out I was a fraud.

Then I saw her. Lilly Ainsworth.

I'd seen her pictures on Instagram. My mom had shown me her profile—she was obsessed with her. Sitting on a luxurious velvet couch, Lilly's reels featured her speaking confidently about alignment and abundance while holding gold-foiled books and a shimmering champagne flute. Honestly, the sheer absurdity of it all had me rolling my eyes. Who lives a life like that? Evidently, *she* did. So she couldn't possibly relate to *my* life.

When she got our attention, I braced myself for the predictable financial pep talk—all those kinds of buzzwords and empty promises I had heard before. My jaw dropped, eyes wide with shock and disbelief, as she recounted getting caught shoplifting at Walmart. I could only imagine the shame and the fear she must have felt. That story, the way she told it, completely caught me off guard. I was speechless.

At that moment, I didn't see the woman radiating confidence who I'd assumed had it all handed to her. I saw a woman who *worked hard* for it. I saw a woman who had once felt exactly like I feel now—ashamed, tired, desperate. A tiny spark of hope ignited within me that maybe she *could* help me.

A heavy silence filled the room after she shared her story, as everyone absorbed her words. She then added, her voice low and steady, "I didn't come here to impress you. I came here to remind you that your past does not define your future. Your mistakes do not determine your worth. And your story—no matter how messy—is the foundation of your magic."

My eyes burned as tears welled up, threatening to spill over. The way she spoke, it was as if the words were meant solely for me. My breath hitched in my throat as I fought to regain control of my emotions. I believed every word.

A hush fell over the room as Lilly paused, her eyes lingering on each of us in turn, the silence heavy with anticipation. She then challenged us. "I've told you my story. Are you ready to share yours?"

My bottom lip trembled as I bit it. I kept my eyes glued to my journal, a blush creeping up my neck as I avoided her gaze. I had been weaving a web of lies for years, deceiving everyone, including myself. How could I possibly share the truth when I don't even know what it is anymore?

"Now is the moment for you to embark on a journey of self-discovery. I have some questions you can answer privately in your journal first, so we can avoid the concern of what everyone else thinks and get closer to the truth," Lilly said, her smile warm and encouraging, her eyes twinkling.

The room filled with the quiet rustle of journals opening, pens uncapping, and the collective intake of breath as everyone prepared to write.

"Alright," she said, smiling gently. "Let's start with something simple—but honest. Who here doesn't love money?"

The room was silent. Everyone looked at each other. No one moved. Except me. My hand trembled as I slowly raised it, though my brain screamed at me to stay silent.

Everyone turned towards me. Not in judgment—more surprised.

My cheeks burned. "I—I don't love money. Not really."

Lilly tilted her head. "Thank you for being brave enough to say that, Sofia. I would love to hear more about it, if you're open to sharing."

I hesitated, my heart pounding in my chest. Everyone leaned forward, waiting for my answer. I wasn't sure what to say. Their gazes felt heavy. I took a slow breath and calmed my racing thoughts. I decided not to overthink it.

"Because it feels like a setup," I said, the words tumbling out before I could filter them. "Like money lures you in with this promise—security, joy, freedom—and then disappears the second you think you're safe. It's like dating a guy who love-bombs you, then ghosts you."

That got a few chuckles. I wasn't trying to be funny, but I was happy to take it.

Lilly gave a soft nod. "That's powerful, Sofia. And painfully relatable."

I shrugged, trying to sound casual, but my voice cracked as I continued.

"Because it never sticks around. I pay off my debt, then something happens, and it's gone again. I work hard—*really* hard—but I always feel behind. I'm tired of feeling like I'm losing a race I didn't even sign up for in the first place, you know?"

"Can anyone else relate to that?" Lilly asked the group.

Several hands went up slowly. Nods. Soft murmurs of agreement.

"If money were a person," she continued. "What kind of relationship would you say you have with it? Write the first thing that comes to mind."

I inhaled sharply. *Toxic* was the word that came to mind. Money and I? We're in a codependent disaster. I want it to save me, but I resent it for not loving me back. I chase it, spend it, punish it, and then wonder why it doesn't stay.

And when she asked what emotions come up when we hear the word "money," I wrote: *Guilt. Fear. Pressure.*

I know I spend too much on frivolous things when I'm stressed or feeling down, and I really need to budget better. Trying to project an image of success is exhausting, and the reality of underearning and overspending just keeps the cycle going. My mom juggles three jobs simultaneously. She doesn't even really seem to enjoy life; she just barely survives! I desperately want to break free of this generational poverty and thrive. I'm just not sure how to do it.

"The first step to prosperity is to look at money as a tool." She paused before continuing. "Not a source of shame. Not a scoreboard. Just a tool."

I bit the inside of my cheek. A tool? That sounds too... peaceful. Money has always felt like a weapon. Like I'm on the wrong end of it. Like it's used to keep people like me small.

But then she said, "What would it feel like to invite money in—not chase it, not fear it—but welcome it with trust?"

For the first time, I envisioned money strolling in casually, like a familiar friend dropping by for a chat. No drama or panic. Just someone who appreciated me and genuinely wanted to spend time with me. With a sigh, I wrote in my journal: *If money were a friend, I'd ask her to stay.*

After waiting for us to finish writing, she asked, "If you could wave a magic wand and remove all guilt, shame, or pressure— what does your dream life look like? Where are you living? What are you doing for work? Who are you with? What are you wearing? What do you truly desire?

In that instant, a vision flooded my senses with such clarity it felt almost tangible. I'm in a sunlit kitchen, the smell of freshly brewed coffee filling the air. I'm barefoot, laughing and sipping espresso with a man who I adore and who adores me. My hair is still curly but shorter, stylish. Outside the French doors, I see our goldendoodle romping in the backyard, his fluffy tail wagging furiously as he chases a bright red ball. A wave of peace and fulfilment washes over me as I watch our baby sleep soundly in my husband's arms.

And money? It's not a stress. It's a quiet presence. Just a nice, steady hum in the background, like a refrigerator keeping everything cool. Financial peace has arrived. No more tears about overdue bills. Plenty of money in the bank.

The vision felt like the sudden, sweet answer to a prayer—a silent wish I hadn't even realized I'd made.

Then Lilly said, "Your financial purpose is not just about a number—it's about who you become when you're living in alignment with your values, your vision, and your worth. What's your first step in that direction?"

My hand hovered over the page. I didn't know what to write. I took a deep breath, and then the words started to flow.

Stop lying to myself.

I stared at the words. And then I underlined them. Because the truth is, something deep down says I'm destined for something more. Not just to own a house, but to belong in a home filled with laughter, love, and family. Not just to find a man, but to find a love that makes me feel worthy and cherished. And not just to make money, but to welcome it with joy and ease.

I looked up and glanced around the circle. Lost in their individual worlds, every woman here wrote intently, revealing their own truths. Despite coming from diverse backgrounds and different stages of life, we were each walking the same path home to ourselves.

When the last woman put her pen down, Lilly spoke. "Let's all take a moment. Close your eyes. And ask yourself: if money were no longer a source of stress, but simply a tool you trusted, what legacy would you create with it? What is your true financial purpose?"

I turned to a fresh page in my journal and wrote at the top: *My Financial Purpose.*

No other words came. I tapped the pen against my thumb, the dull click echoing in the quiet room. Frustration bubbled up. I'd done the affirmations. Read *You Are a Badass at Making Money* three times. Listened to the podcasts. I even cut out takeout coffee for six whole weeks. And yet I was still broke, living in my mom's basement with maxed-out credit cards, buying things I didn't even want.

Maybe I'm just not meant for wealth, I thought.

But then Lilly's voice came back to me. "Money is not the goal—it's the tool. Your financial purpose is your goal. What is the impact you want money to make in your life?"

I closed my eyes and let my imagination wander. The scene I'd imagined earlier, a loving family in the kitchen, came flooding back to me. What else could I possibly desire? I inhaled deeply, the question hanging heavy in the air. I opened my eyes and wrote:

My financial purpose is to feel independent and at peace.

I want to do work that lights me up.

I want to give back—to help young girls from single-parent homes feel confident and capable.

Wait. *What?* Where did that idea come from?

For years, I've been so focused on myself and what I wanted that I never considered anyone else. The moment felt electric, as if a switch flipped inside me, unveiling a truth I never knew existed. The old uncertainty was gone, replaced with such clarity.

I wrote: *I want to learn to truly thrive in every way so I can empower young girls to achieve their dreams.* Feeling the depth of that intention, my eyes welled up and my breath hitched in my throat.

"You don't have to wait on money to make your dreams come true. You can act on it now. What can you do now to start living out your life's dream?" Lilly challenged.

What's the very first thing to do? I used to think, *when I have my own money, I will...* or *when I have a partner...* but this feeling of purpose is about something more. If this is what I want to do, how can I start now from where I am? Instead of that usual gnawing fear associated with money, I felt a lightness, a sense of calm I hadn't experienced before. It really is a tool to bring my vision to life.

My financial purpose. For the first time, it felt real. Like something I could hold on to when the fear crept in. I looked down at the last line I had written: *I want to learn to truly thrive in every way so I can empower young girls to achieve their dreams.* I felt a quiet determination setting in.

I thought of my younger self—quiet, unsure, watching my mom come home exhausted from one of many long shifts, too tired to talk about money or dreams. Instead of wondering what I wanted, people only cared about how I'd manage, a constant pressure of survival dulling any spark of personal ambition. I don't want anyone else to experience that.

I don't have to wait until I'm rich to start giving back, I wrote, surprised by my own words. I can build a life—and a business— that helps others while I grow.

I paused. For the first time in a long time, the idea of money made me feel excited! Not because I wanted more stuff—but because I saw how money could finally become a bridge to meaning. My first step is to own my value for those young women who are following behind me. I can help them. I can make a difference. My face broke into a broad, beaming smile, my shoulders rising in a happy response.

"How many of you are surprised with your answers?" Lilly asked.

Every hand shot up in a wave of agreement, and I felt a surge of relief seeing they had the same shift as me.

"Today, during our midday break, I want you to find a beautiful space to sit, think, feel, and journal about this. Your financial purpose is not just about a number—it's about who you become when you're living in alignment with your values, your vision, and your worth. Think about who you are when you are living with purpose. And what is one action step you can take while you are here to move you closer to that version of you?"

I carefully wrote down the question before closing my eyes. With a deep breath, I felt the strength of this new Sofia settle over me, and I vowed to honor her. *I can totally do this,* I thought.

And, for the first time in a long time, a surge of excitement, determination, and purpose filled me up, ready to see my life differently.

***

Are you ready to declare your financial purpose?
You can locate the exercise on page 199.

Chapter 6

Shift Your Money Mindset

Barb

The hotel mirror didn't lie: Every line and imperfection was starkly visible.

The cold porcelain sink pressed against my clammy palms as I stood rigid before it, clinging to the bathroom counter's edge for support. My hair—short, wispy, stubborn—had finally grown back in. The chemo had taken more than my health. It had stolen my femininity, leaving me feeling vulnerable. A wave of self-doubt washed over me, crushing my fragile sense of self-worth and leaving me feeling anything but confident. I ran a hand over the soft bristle of sandy brown hair that had shaped into something like a pixie cut. Compared to being bald, it was an improvement, but seeing my hair so short still surprised me. It had been so long since I had looked in the mirror and truly saw myself with a sense of familiarity and acceptance.

From the open balcony doors, the green, earthy scent of the palm trees and the perfume of jasmine mixed with the sharp, clean smell of the expensive hotel soap that was such a luxury for me. Back home, I'd always bought whatever was on sale. Every purchase was practical, and I deliberated every financial decision.

Until now.

I heard the women in the office lunchroom whispering about

Lilly Ainsworth like she was some kind of money goddess in high heels. One of them held up her new book like it was sacred, her voice practically vibrating with devotion.

"She's the real deal," the woman had said. "My credit score is up, my confidence is up, and I swear I'm finally dating like I'm not afraid to be seen."

Annoyed, I rolled my eyes. There is no way that could be true.

But that night, alone in my recliner with a half-finished jigsaw puzzle and my cat draped across my thighs, the conversation replayed in my mind. My body seemed to move without conscious direction, and without a second thought, I ordered the book.

The day it arrived, I couldn't put it down; I read the whole thing in one sitting. Lilly's words resonated deeply. Not just the advice, but the tone, like she was speaking directly to me. She pushed past the hard outer shell and into the part of me that still wanted to *feel*. To live. To have a life beyond this.

I searched for her on Instagram, eager to see what kind of life she presented to the world. I don't follow many people, mostly just yarn shops and cat rescues. But there she was in a cream blouse and jeans, standing in front of a fountain in Bali, saying, "If you're tired of being safe and lonely, this is your invitation."

Before I could second-guess my decision, my finger hit the "Book Now" button. Then a sudden realization—a confusing mix of shock and self-doubt—hit me hard. What had I just done? Who on earth have I become? I was so embarrassed that I didn't tell anyone, not even my sister.

When I requested vacation time, my boss's worried frown and questioning gaze made me wonder if I'd made a mistake. Before my cancer diagnosis, the idea of a vacation was a distant dream, a luxury I'd never allowed myself. There was no place I really wanted to go, and I'd rather have the vacation pay at the end of the year. I even hated taking the time off for my treatments. It felt more like a punishment than a benefit. My government job filled both my days and my bank account, so the thought of a reduced paycheck because I was sick filled me with a terrifying blend of financial anxiety and the prospect of soul-crushing boredom.

And now, standing in a Balinese hotel room in front of a mirror that showed me every inch of my new, vulnerable, unfamiliar self, I wondered if I was out of my mind. *This* may be worse than the chemotherapy.

The sounds of birds singing blended with the sounds of waves crashing. Everything around me looked like it belonged on a postcard. I should have felt a deep, overwhelming sense of gratitude and joy, but I didn't. The decision to come here, so out of character, left me with a strong sense of regret and a nervous flutter in my stomach, a feeling completely outside my comfort zone. Having already paid the non-refundable retreat fees, I felt no option but to attend; I wasn't going to waste the money I'd spent. So I convinced myself that I was there to gain invaluable financial expertise that would make this trip more than worth it. I walked out of my room and made my way down to the meeting room, determined to be just a witness, not a participant.

Entering the room, I felt like I'd walked onto the set of a fashion magazine. Every woman was beautiful and stylish, with picture-perfect outfits. Lilly Ainsworth stood at the front, impeccably dressed and radiating confidence. In the oppressive heat, my comfy cargo shorts, cool linen shirt, and well-worn Birkenstocks felt like a sensible, though not stylish, choice. The stark contrast to the other women made me feel painfully out of place. Head down, I quietly found my table, sat down, and looked at the journal sitting in front of me. I survived cancer, so surely, I can survive this. All I need to do is stay quiet and listen.

The room fell silent as Lilly recounted her shocking story of shoplifting, the details creating a vivid image in my mind. As her words hung in the air, a wave of understanding washed over me, instantly changing my perception of Lilly. She wasn't perfect. And she knew how it felt to overcome something difficult.

Then Sofia, with a brave heart, shared her story. Just imagining myself sharing personal details with this group triggered me. The idea of being vulnerable in this way was something I was actively trying to avoid during this retreat.

When we went our separate ways midday, I spent a peaceful lunch break sitting alone on a bench overlooking the ocean, the sound of crashing waves a soothing backdrop to my work on Lilly's questions. It was odd, but with each word I wrote, a sense of trust blossomed within me—a quiet confidence, a fragile hope taking root. How is it that I'm feeling so different in just a few short hours?

Once we had gathered again after the lunch break, Lilly said, "Let's move on to the next tenet of Sacred Prosperity. Raise your hand if money feels like your safety net, but also your prison?"

My arm shot up involuntarily, faster than my mind could process. My mind caught up to the action, and a hot blush immediately rose from my chest to my cheeks, burning them a crimson red.

As her head turned towards me, the kindness in her eyes melted away my embarrassment. Lilly's smile, radiating warmth, made me feel at ease.

"Barb?"

Unsure of what I was supposed to say, I hesitated. A wave of anxiety washed over me as my heart pounded in my chest. Then the words spilled out. "I've always saved. It's what I know. I don't really... spend. I guess it feels safer that way. My parents were farmers who saved everything because the harvest might fail. You didn't ask questions. You just prepared. So I did the same thing even though I have had the same job for the past twenty-five years with the same salary. Even now, when I have more than a million dollars in the bank, I can't seem to do anything different."

There were nods. Kind eyes. No judgment. But I still wanted to disappear.

Lilly stepped closer, her voice kind. "Barb, what you just shared is incredibly powerful. You were taught that money must be protected. That spending is dangerous. That thought created a feeling: fear. And that feeling of fear drove your actions of hoarding, clinging to your money, and staying small." Lilly paused for a moment to let that sink in. "And as a result... you are safe. Congratulations on fulfilling your parents' wishes. But you are also stuck in a life that you are not really living."

I swallowed hard. It was like Lilly had cracked open a secret chamber I hadn't realized was locked.

Lilly turned to the group. "Research has shown that we learn many of our beliefs about money by the age of seven, through our family, friends, culture, and our environment. This is how we create a life we didn't want or consciously choose. Our thoughts, often unconscious, create our feelings. Those feelings drive our actions, and the actions create our results. So, you need to figure out the underlying thoughts before you can change any actions that determine your world. And here's something important," Lilly said, her voice dropping as if she were sharing a sacred truth. "Women, especially, often seek safety first with money. We're taught to be careful and cautious and to protect ourselves. And there's nothing wrong with building a sound foundation. But if safety becomes a cage, not a launch pad, then money isn't serving you anymore. You are serving it." Lilly took a breath, letting the words settle.

Something shifted in my chest. Then a tightness, a pressure built up in my throat. What is she saying? I've always considered myself independent, capable of handling challenges, and making my own decisions without relying on others. I have my job, my little apartment, and my cats. But I never considered that maybe I wasn't free. Was this quiet life really a cage?

Then she asked me to imagine something I'd never allowed myself to think about.

"Barb," she said, "what if your money wasn't meant to be locked away? What if it could create friendships? Joy? Beauty? Impact? What would that look like for you? You have already created safety. You've already won that game. Now, what else could you create if you trusted your money to support you, not just protect you?

I didn't know how to answer. "I've never thought about money creating anything other than safety. But maybe... maybe I would like to have a genuine friend. Or take a class, or go somewhere new, or even volunteer."

Then Lilly spoke, her words holding such profound truth that it startled me to my core.

"You're standing on the dance floor, Barb, holding your partner— money—so tightly that neither of you can move. It's time to trust the music. To move. To let your money flow."

I opened my mouth to speak, but the words caught in my throat, leaving me speechless. That way of thinking about money was entirely new to me. Dancing is not something I typically do, but something inside me—something old and quiet and aching— wanted to. Just a little.

"Let go, Barb," Lilly said to me. "I'm here to help you relax and enjoy the dance. And the rest of you," she said, sweeping her arm before the group. "This is one of my favorite ways to help women like all of you to let go of the nagging anxieties of scarcity and fear, and instead embrace the joyful, abundant dance with money. In fact, this is the homework for all of you tonight. I want you to write down all of the things you would allow yourself to experience if you trusted money to support you."

"Because tomorrow," Lilly said, her eyes sparkling, "we're going to take this from paper to practice. A small but powerful step—a chance to step into the energy of joyful receiving and experience what it feels like to let money support your delight."

And then, with a gleam in her eye, she told us all about the luxury spending day we'd experience tomorrow, a day dedicated to indulging in life's finer things.

My stomach twisted.

Lilly looked at me as she spoke.

"This isn't about recklessness," she said. "This is about reclaiming joy. About practicing these new thoughts: *Money is safe—and so is joy. Money flows to me and through me for good. I am worthy of beauty, connection, and delight.* Even if you only spend a little. Even if it feels awkward. Actually, especially if it feels awkward."

The words felt too big. But they also felt... possible. Maybe I could walk into a store and feel free, abundant. Even if I bought nothing, I could still enjoy browsing through the shops. Or what if I bought something just for the sake of it, something not practical, yet deeply satisfying, an act of self-indulgence that would bring a smile to my face?

That night, I couldn't sleep. Standing on the balcony, I whispered into the darkness, "What if I could trust money to give me more than safety? What if I could trust myself with joy? I've got a second chance at life. Isn't it about time?"

I wrapped my fingers around the railing, feeling the weight of years of old beliefs—and the first flicker of something new.

Possibility.

***

Ready to shift your money beliefs? Proceed to page 201.

Chapter 7

Your Wealthy Self-Image

Mikayla

I slid out of bed, pushing back the cool sheets clinging to my legs, and padded barefoot across the teak wood floor towards the mirror. Bali's light is uniquely soft and golden, like honey, warming everything it touches. My deep brown skin glowed, warm and rich under its light. I leaned closer, the reflection in my brown eyes catching the light, and I saw the golden specks dance and sparkle. With a swipe, my smudged mascara disappeared. Running a finger through the soft, springy curls around my face, I wondered how I'd ended up here—on the other side of the world, at a wealth retreat that had drained my bank account.

If Lilly can't help me, I'll have to move back in with my parents.

The thought twisted my stomach into a nauseous knot of anxiety and shame. To get my head above water, I'd have to sell everything I owned. How do I sell my condo after all the hard work and effort I put into getting it? Especially with the extravagant, custom-built, walk-in closet that's straight out of a *Real Housewives'* episode. My beamer, a dream car since my teenage years, still makes my heart race the moment I push the ignition. But let's be realistic. None of it was really mine now. Stuffed in a drawer at home were notices of overdue payments and threats of repossession.

Despite my parents' doubts about my ambition and ability, I made a million dollars. *A million!* And then I spent it, gloriously, with reckless abandon on clothes, shoes, and expensive perfume. Deep down, a quiet voice always whispered that it wouldn't last. And maybe that's the painful truth I didn't want to acknowledge. On some deep level, I always believed I'd lose it.

When I saw Lilly's Instagram post about the retreat, I didn't think twice; I booked it immediately. Me—who usually spends an hour meticulously choosing a lip color, agonizing over shades and finishes—booked an international flight in under six minutes. I was that desperate. Lilly is my last hope, and I don't know what I'll do if she fails me.

I walked to the closet, my eyes scanning the outfits hanging neatly, searching for something appropriate for our second day. We were asked to wear comfortable athletic wear, like yoga pants and t-shirts. I pulled on my favorite Lululemon tank, the vibrant blue a cheerful start to the day, and the matching capris. The material was buttery soft against my skin. Looking in the mirror, I could see the fit was perfect; they even made my butt look fantastic.

With meticulous precision, I applied my makeup, blending it into a soft, warm glow against my smooth skin. The result was flawless—airbrushed, like the women in magazines. This ritual was more than vanity. It was survival. If I could look the part, perfectly put-together, maybe no one would see the desperation gnawing at my insides.

My phone buzzed with a jarring reminder that it was time to leave. Shit. I hadn't touched my hair. A quick glance in the mirror reassured me. Even after sleeping, my hair was almost perfect. Thank God! I squeezed a dab of coconut-scented hair gloss on my palm, rubbed my hands together, then ran them over my hair, and I was done.

I rushed out the door and down the winding path toward the retreat space, breath catching from the heat.

The open-air pavilion was alive with the murmur of voices, the cheerful sound of laughter, and the delicate scent of flowers. The stiff, uncomfortable atmosphere of the previous day was gone, and warm smiles and welcoming gazes greeted me from the women who sat cross-legged on plump, orange meditation cushions in a semicircle.

Lilly stood at the front, talking to Katie, who had led the meditation yesterday afternoon. Her presence was magnetic even in quiet conversation. She wore a white cotton tunic with a gold leaf pattern stitched on it and matching capri pants underneath. Even in casual clothes, Lilly crushed fashion. For a moment, I just watched her—this woman I had followed online for years, admired from afar, envied, adored, maybe even resented a little. And now, here I was at her event.

Yesterday, in the first moments of the retreat, she launched into her true story about shoplifting from Walmart, a desperate act committed during her tough years as a young, overwhelmed single mother. And she didn't just mention it like some polished TED Talk confession. It was raw, visceral, and filled with emotion.

Something shifted in me. This wasn't a showy display meant to gain our admiration—it was heartfelt and real. It didn't make me think less of her. In fact, I admired her strength and perseverance. By bravely revealing her most painful experience, she showed us that vulnerability wasn't weakness, but a path to connection.

But I didn't know what to do with all that vulnerability and honesty; it felt like a raw, exposed nerve. A code of silence reigned in my house. My parents firmly believed that family matters were strictly confidential and never discussed outside the home. Tears and complaints were considered signs of weakness, so you should never reveal them. And don't you dare share the truth with a room full of strangers! Instinctively, I shivered at the thought.

Clearly, not every participant felt the same. Sofia was the first to raise her hand. Tears welled in her eyes, but she didn't hesitate to share her emotional story. Barb, the woman who wore the linen shirt and shorts, was next. Though more reserved, she still shared a surprising amount, her words carefully chosen. It was insane to think that she had a million dollars in the bank. I looked down at my carefully curated outfit and over at her and shook my head. Never judge a book by its cover. Never. My mother's words felt so weighty, so undeniably true. Obviously, it wasn't easy for them to share, but they spoke about themselves with such bravery and authenticity, I admired them.

I approached an open spot and settled onto the comfortable cushion between Barb and another woman, Zoe. In unison, they both said "hi," followed by a chorus of nervous giggles and smiles at their coordinated greeting.

"Good morning," I responded, laughing with them. I set my journal and water bottle down beside me just as Lilly started to speak.

"Welcome to Day Two, everyone! Day One was epic, filled with unforgettable moments, and a shared sense of transformation—wouldn't you all agree?" I looked around, seeing quiet nods of agreement.

"Well, Day Two is going to be even better," she said, a grin spreading across her face. "These steps I'm teaching you are cumulative; each one adds to the complexity and understanding of the previous steps. Think of it as a ladder, where each step brings you closer to your purpose. In order to reach the last step at the top, you must first place your foot on the bottom rung. But there is also the process of integration. It involves transferring the knowledge and understanding from your mind to your heart. That is the way we reprogram the subconscious mind and create lasting change. Before we begin, we need to drop into our bodies. Meditation helps us do that—by calming the noise in our minds, shifting us from thinking into feeling, and preparing us to receive what's next. Let's give a warm welcome again to Katie." Lilly started the round of applause before finding her cushion and getting comfortable on it.

Katie, a small Balinese woman with a gentle smile and bright eyes, stepped up to the front of the circle. She was petite, no more than five feet tall, her dark chestnut hair neatly pulled back into a side bun, adorned with a cheerful yellow flower. Her white linen tunic, flawlessly simple, contrasted beautifully with the deep royal blue of her flowing skirt, which featured an intricate light-blue leaf pattern.

"Hello again, everyone. I'm deeply honored to guide you through this morning's meditation session, helping you find your inner peace and calm. This creates the space for renewal. Ready to begin?" Katie said, the melodic rise and fall of her accent adding warmth to her words.

I settled onto my cushion, trying to mirror the ease of the women around me, but my spine felt rigid and my jaw was tight. Katie sat at the front, poised and serene, her presence calm like still water. This was my first time meditating, and already I was squirming inside.

Sitting still was hard for me. I'm the kind of person who keeps moving—deadlines, scrolling, cleaning—anything to stay one step ahead of my anxiety. Now, in this silent circle, there was nowhere to run. Katie invited us to let the teachings of the *Rise Into Prosperity* retreat settle into our bodies. To connect with our breath. To be still. I closed my eyes, but my mind didn't follow. Thoughts pinballed from one corner to another—what I should've said yesterday, how much this retreat had cost, whether I was even supposed to be here. The same loops, circling back again and again. I peeked at the others, so composed, so inward. I tried again. Inhale. Exhale. Maybe I didn't need to quiet my mind perfectly. Maybe just being here was enough—for now.

With the meditation complete, Katie instructed us to stand and shake off any remaining emotion that did not serve us, leaving me feeling lighter and more peaceful. The session closed with a quiet Balinese prayer, before she bowed with her hands pressed together in front of her chest respectfully, saying, "*Om Swastiastu*—may you be blessed and protected."

Collectively, we instinctively mirrored her bow and responded: "Om Swastiastu."

Lilly stepped to the front again, stood beside Katie, and turned to her. "Thank you so much, Katie. You are such an important part of the work we are doing this week. I look forward to having you back tomorrow for breathwork." She gently touched Katie's arm and smiled. "I always feel so much better after doing your sessions." She turned to us and said, "Do you all agree?"

A few of us nodded, and several answered, "Yes."

"We are going to take a ten-minute hydration break, and then we'll get back at it. Please take your cushions and put them along the wall out of the way before you grab a drink."

She bent down, grabbed her own cushion and Katie's, walked over to the left of the refreshment table, and tucked them up against the wall.

One by one, we all did the same. Then, some went out to find the restroom while the rest of us filled our coffee cups.

"After that, I have so much energy, I'm not sure I need any caffeine," Zoe said, standing beside Barb and me.

"I was so nervous!" Barb said, laughing. "I'm not sure I relaxed enough to say the same."

"Thank God I wasn't the only one," I answered, letting out a breath I didn't realize I was holding. "This is so out of my comfort zone."

"Same," Barb said, smiling at me.

"You were so amazing sharing your story yesterday," I said. "How could breathwork faze you?" I asked.

"Thanks for reminding me of *that*. I was hoping everyone would wake up with amnesia and forget I said anything yesterday. Although..." she paused. "I felt a hundred pounds lighter after sharing. I didn't realize I was carrying around such a burden. And I have to say, you look so confident and put together, I wouldn't think anything would faze *you*."

"I'm with you on that, Barb," Zoe chimed in.

"Thanks," I said, not knowing what else to say. Should I tell them that while I'm an expert at looking good, my life is hell? Or, should I share that I've spent hours perfecting my makeup and years learning how to conceal my emotions? Feeling awkward, I smiled and said, "I guess we'd better go to our seats."

When we were all seated, Lilly stood at the front of the semicircle.

"Before we begin today's lesson, I want to express my gratitude to Sofia and Barb for their openness and honesty during yesterday's discussion. This container is not exclusive to one person; it is a shared experience among many. We gather as a community of sacred beings, and our purpose is to listen, support, and learn together. Was anyone else here besides me deeply affected by what those two shared?"

I gave Barb a quick nod and a friendly smile. A chorus of yeses and subtle nods rippled through the rest of the women. Some even started a few hesitant claps of applause before trailing off awkwardly.

"Don't stop," Lilly said. "They deserve applause for their courage."

A thunderous applause erupted as we all started clapping. I noticed both Barb and Sofia, their faces flushed, a mixture of bashful embarrassment and quiet pride. A small, almost imperceptible smile tugged at Sofia's lips. Barb, however, offered a wide, exaggerated grin, her eyes rolling playfully in her head.

"Well done, both of you," she said, first looking at Sofia and then Barb. "This is a safe space where you can share your story so you can grow," she continued, turning back to us all. "Today, we are covering one of my favorite things to teach. It is all about discovering you are worthy of anything and everything you desire in life."

Worthy? If I were worthy, I wouldn't be facing this impossible situation. I felt the emotion building, a tightness in my chest, a lump in my throat.

It was the familiar sting of frustration and constant anxiety of missed payments and dwindling resources.

Then Lilly said something that stole the breath from my lungs.

"A wealthy self-image isn't just about what you wear or what you drive. It's who you believe you are, and more importantly, how deeply you feel that truth when no one's watching. Do you believe you're worthy of wealth?" She paused and looked at each of us in turn. "Do you trust yourself to keep it, grow it, and circulate it with joy?"

Do I trust myself to keep it, grow it, and circulate wealth with joy? Ummm... no. A hard no, in fact.

I learned at such an early age not to cry in front of strangers, so the tears spilling down my cheeks shocked me. Lilly saw me and walked towards me.

"Mikayla? Would you be open to sharing?"

I took a breath. Big mistake. My throat seized like it didn't want the words to come out.

Lilly's touch was light as a feather on my arm, her other hand gently lifting the small, branded pocket mirror from my table. The latch clicked as she opened it, and then she handed it to me.

"When you look in the mirror, who do you see?"

I thought for a minute. My throat was so tight, I could barely breathe, and I cleared it nervously. "I see a woman who looks expensive," I said, letting the edge into my voice, "but still feels cheap inside." I took a shallow breath and shook my head from side to side. "I see the girl with the lashes and the Louis Vuitton bag, the one who never shows up in sweatpants or without lip gloss." Drawing in a deep breath, I continued. "But behind all that? I see someone who's terrified of not being good enough."

Lilly nodded encouragingly. "Not good enough for what?"

"For any of it," I said. "The condo. The car. The money. I made seven figures as a coach before I turned thirty, but now, I'm completely broke. I bought shoes, went to lavish parties, and on luxury vacations... You name it. I told myself I was living the dream—but really, I was trying to outrun the nightmare."

Lilly's hand, warm and comforting, settled on my shoulder; her gentle squeeze was a silent message of support. "What's the nightmare, Mikayla?"

I could barely say it.

"My dad being right," I said, the weight of the words pressing down on me. "You should have seen the way he looked at me when I got my BMW, like I had betrayed him just by succeeding. And he told me it would never last because I was *his* daughter, and we didn't live that way. The nightmare... It's the chilling reality that he might be right, and I'll be back in my parents' basement, a complete failure."

Lilly's voice dropped. "And if that happened, what would it mean about you?"

A lump caught in my throat. I swallowed hard and answered, "That I'm not good enough and I never was."

I could feel the other women leaning in for support. One wiped away a tear from her cheek.

"I wasn't buying things," I continued. "I was buying space between me and the little girl in hand-me-down clothes who cowered in the closet when her parents argued with frustration and fear over the unpaid bills and the reality of an empty refrigerator. My plan was that if I just looked perfect, with flawless makeup and the right clothes, no one would ever guess I was her. So, I poured my heart into work, earned every penny, and blew it all on anything I could to show everyone I wasn't."

"And what do you believe about wealth now?" Lilly asked.

"That it's a trick mirror." I slammed the pocket mirror shut and looked up at her. "It shows you what you want to see—until it shatters."

Lilly looked at me with something more than compassion. It was like she knew how that felt.

"Mikayla," she said, "what if wealth isn't about accumulation, but about embodiment? Who you *own* yourself to be, even before the evidence shows up."

I stared at her. "What do you mean?"

"Your wealthy self-image," she said, "isn't the designer wardrobe. It's not the condo. It's the version of you who no longer has to prove she's worthy because she *already* knows she is. She loves all parts of herself, the fierce and the fragile, the polished and the messy. She doesn't need permission. She just *is*."

I closed my eyes, a wave of heat rising to my cheeks, and exhaled slowly, embarrassed by everything I'd shared. *Damn*, I thought. *Lilly is good at this.*

Lilly kept on. "What three words would your inner critic use to describe you?"

I didn't open my eyes. I could feel the weight of everyone's gaze, their silence a heavy pressure as they waited for my answer. My voice was barely a whisper. "Selfish. Fake. Failure."

"And your future self, the one who's grown through it?"

"Brave. Free. Enough." I said without even thinking. I exhaled as the words repeated in my mind and opened my eyes.

With a subtle nod, Lilly turned and walked toward the front of the room. "Let's dig deeper. I want everyone to take a moment, open your journals, and write down this question: What money-related beliefs did your parents pass on to you?" She waited patiently until we had finished writing. Then, her head tilted, she slowly turned to face me. "Mikayla... would you be open to sharing what came up for you?"

I didn't hesitate. "Money is hard. There's never enough. Money makes people angry. It's why Dad left and why Mom cried. Rich people are greedy and cold. And people like us, we got the scraps. Nothing more."

Lilly paused, letting the weight of my words hang in the air and giving me a moment to catch my breath. "Are those beliefs still running the show?"

"They are the whole damn production."

The group let out a quiet chuckle. I wiped my face, smiling a little through the mess.

Lilly smiled. "Then maybe it's time to rewrite the story. Look in the mirror again." She paused.

I grabbed the case, flipped it open, and looked back at my reflection.

"Who do you see now?"

I paused and looked deep into my own eyes. "I see someone who is tired of playing a role instead of living her life. I see someone who is lonely, exhausted, and scared."

"Who do you want to see? Speak from your heart," Lilly pushed.

I closed my eyes for a moment. The question echoed in my mind. *Who do I want to see?* I opened my eyes and took a moment to study my reflection. "Someone who doesn't have to pretend. Someone who wakes up peaceful, not panicked. Someone who knows— really knows—that she's enough, with or without the shoes, the beamer, the friends, the lifestyle." I looked up from the mirror and searched Lilly's face, desperate for any flicker of hope.

Lilly smiled. "And when you had all the money you ever wanted?"

"Even when I had it, I was still that little girl at the kitchen table watching her mother quietly count change for the bus. I was still proving something. Still terrified that I would end up back in that house. And here I am now, practically already there."

"And if it is all gone, who are you?"

I swallowed. Would there be anything left of me? I don't know. That scared me more than being broke. "I don't know," I sighed.

"Okay, let's back up a step, Mikayla. Where in your life do you keep proving you're not your parents, but still living the same story emotionally?"

"I've built this life around *not being them*. Not poor. Not small. Not invisible. Not sad. But the fear? The scarcity? It's all still there. Different packaging, but the same damn story."

Lilly stood and turned to the whole group. "This is why I do this work. Not just to help you build wealth—but to help you rise. To learn from what was, grow into what's possible, and expand into the woman you're here to be. To finally make peace with your story, your choices, and your becoming."

"If you want to attract sustainable wealth, you must believe you are someone who can hold it. You must see yourself as worthy. Not perfect. Not finished. Just worthy."

Then she looked back at me.

"Mikayla, what if you didn't lose your wealth—you just spent it on the wrong identity?"

My breath caught. *What? The wrong identity?* I let that sink into my brain, the words echoing softly in my mind.

"Then maybe I didn't fail," I said. "Maybe I was just building the version of me who would finally stop hiding."

"Yes, that's it, Mikayla! Maybe you made the best investment of all... priceless in fact." She addressed the group. "I want you all to place a hand on your heart."

All of us raised our hands to our hearts.

"Picture her," she said. "Your wealthy self. What does she look like? What is she wearing? What does she value? How does she speak to herself? How does she walk through a room?"

I closed my eyes. She is radiant. Makeup and hair flawless. Standing tall, still wearing heels. Her eyes are softer. Her laugh is genuine, and her heart is open. She is exuding confidence because she finally loves who she is. All of *her!*

"Now, let's write down this image you have just created in your mind. It is the first step to making it real."

I opened my eyes, and for the first time in a long time, I didn't feel like a fraud. I felt like a woman becoming whole.

***

To write your wealthy self-image script, go to page 203 to get started.

Chapter 8

Worthy By Design

Zoe

By the time we took our lunch break, I was still thinking about Mikayla's story.

The tremor in her voice as she confessed to squandering all her money, the vulnerability in her admission, awakened a deep empathy within me. I hadn't expected such raw, unflinching honesty. Especially not from someone like her, dripping in confidence and designer labels. I assumed she had had it all together.

But she didn't.

And that... that was strangely comforting.

She spoke of a childhood marked by poverty coupled with the weight of shame. She shared how she tried to bury those roots, that deep-seated part of herself, beneath a carefully constructed image of wealth and status. Each strategy that she meticulously crafted to keep the ruse going had failed because deep down, she still felt unworthy.

It was like she was telling a version of my story—just with different characters and a discounted wardrobe.

Over lunch, Mikayla, Barb, Sofia, and I shared a quiet moment, the clinking of silverware as a gentle backdrop to our conversation about the freedom of finally speaking our truths without fear of judgment. From the guarded silences of Day One, the group had evolved into a collaborative, open environment, buzzing with shared experiences and mutual support. A warmth spread through me, a feeling of belonging, and it made me smile.

Afterward, Lilly gathered us for what she called the "Luxury Shopping Experience."

The name alone made my stomach tighten.

"This isn't about spending money," Lilly insisted. "This exercise is about stepping into that self-image you created earlier. It is about confronting your money habits and behaviors, pushing you past your subconscious and conscious limitations. It is time to face your feelings of guilt, shame, and low self-worth by observing how you actually restrict yourself or spend money." She made sure everyone was listening before continuing. "You are not buying an item today; you are meeting a part of yourself: The one who believes she is allowed to receive."

That hit me hard. My parents taught me that money was a resource reserved for bills, children, and emergencies, not for personal indulgence. It took me drowning in wine and loneliness to lose all restraint and carelessly spend money on things I didn't need. Then the guilt and regret would hit me like a ton of bricks, a sickening feeling in the pit of my stomach, and the joy of the purchase would be gone, making me feel like I had failed again.

But this... this was different. This was sober, conscious, intentional.

After a twenty-minute van ride, Lilly led us into an exclusive shopping district. I decided on the trip there that I could bluff my way through the experience by pretending to browse, running my fingers over the luxurious silk scarves, or spritzing a perfume and then calling it a day without spending any money at all.

Then Lilly said, "I want you to walk this path on your own. That way, there will be no influence from others. This needs to come from within you. And you must buy something. The amount you spend is not important. This is about expanding your comfort level and stretching into possibility. Allow yourself to lean into trust. What matters is that it sparks joy, as Marie Kondo says."

So much for not buying anything.

Every store was an expensive luxury brand, the windows displaying dazzling, high-end merchandise. In my cheap floral dress from Walmart, I felt utterly out of place among the silk and designer labels. I felt so unsure of myself, as I did in my marriage, asking for permission to matter.

I wandered aimlessly for an hour. Then I bumped into Mikayla, her face radiant as she tried on designer sunglasses; their price tag made my grocery bill look like pocket change. Later, I saw Barb—and had to do a double-take. She stood in front of a full-length mirror wearing a flowing silk batik dress in deep indigo and copper—the traditional Balinese patterns swirling like ocean currents across the fabric. She looked radiant, confident and... sexy.

I wandered through shop after shop, unsure what I was even looking for. I saw luxurious silk robes in jewel tones, fragrant spa oils, and leather-bound handmade journals. Beautiful things. But none of them called out to me.

Thirty minutes remained, and the weight of each step grew heavier as I felt mired in defeat. Every rack I flipped through felt like a reminder that I didn't belong here—that this wasn't my world. I could already picture the rest of the women's shopping bags clutched with pride, their laughter on the bus, the casual, *Oh, Zoe didn't buy anything?* And Lilly—what would she think? That I wasn't open enough? That I'd failed the exercise? I was already rehearsing excuses when something in the corner of my eye grabbed my attention.

Nestled between two upscale boutiques, a tiny storefront with a hand-painted sign peeked out. *Kismet.* The name sparkled above the door in gold script, a delicate blue butterfly, wings dusted with iridescent glitter, rested in the corner like a secret invitation.

I stepped closer. A dazzling collection of rings and pendants, each distinct from the next, was displayed in the window case. Some of the gemstones are rough and wild. Others had been polished until they gleamed, their smoothness a stark contrast to the rougher stones nearby. Each one looked like it carried a story.

Something about the window—those delicate pieces glinting in the light, that blue butterfly—called to me. It wasn't logical. It was a pull, quiet but insistent, like some invisible thread had just tugged at my chest. Before I knew it, my hand was on the door. And then I stepped inside.

The air was cool and scented with something sweet and ancient— jasmine, maybe, or rosewood. A woman behind the counter looked up and smiled warmly, like she had been expecting me.

"Can I help you find something?"

I opened my mouth, but panic rose in my chest. The price tags. God, the prices. I didn't belong here.

"I—I'm just looking," I stammered.

She smiled and tilted her head. Her gaze didn't hold any judgment, no hint that I was out of place. "Please feel free to spend as much time as you like; there's no rush, and you can relax and enjoy the experience. I feel like this store is like an art gallery. The experience demands a slow, careful appreciation; you'll want to savor each piece, taking in its colors, its form, its quiet power. If you see anything that catches your eye, or have questions, please don't hesitate to ask."

"I'm looking for a ring," I blurted. "Something to mark my divorce. My freedom. I guess... a reminder of coming back to myself."

Her smile widened, crinkling the corners of her eyes. "I know exactly the one," she said, walking to a glass case that shimmered under the light and lifting out a velvet tray filled with rings of every shape and size.

The most breathtaking ring I had ever seen lay in the middle of the tray, its intricate design catching my eye. The polished gold gleamed warmly, its surface reflecting the light, and a bold diamond shape dominated its face. At its center was a soft, dreamy blue stone, like a beautiful tropical sky, shimmering with an inner light.

"Larimar is a rare and beautiful stone," she said, her eyes gleaming. "You can only find it in a remote, mountainous region of the Dominican Republic. It's said to soothe the heart, calm the soul, and awaken the divine feminine. An Australian artist created this ring, etching the band with symbols for self-trust, new beginnings, and inner light. It was blessed with the powerful affirmation: *You are worthy.*"

I stood there, mesmerized by the ring's beauty and the way the light caught the stone. A feeling washed over me that it was meant to be mine. I slipped it on. A perfect fit. This was more than a ring. It was a declaration. And I didn't want to take it off.

But when she told me the price, my stomach twisted. I could get a basic silver ring for twenty dollars down the street and could easily pay for it by skipping dinner out one night. Repaying this amount would take months, if not a year. I calculated how I could make up this money in the next three months, my mind racing with possibilities and anxieties. No more takeout. No more extras at all. Was it worth it?

In one heartbeat, I heard my mother's voice: *You cannot have that.* Then, in the next, I heard Lilly's: *What if your wealth begins the moment you believe you're worthy?*

I took a deep breath and stood tall. My eyes narrowed, and I chewed on my bottom lip. Worthy. Am I worthy? Damn right I am. I've been through hell, and yet I'm still standing.

My hand trembled as I reached into my wallet for my credit card. I hesitated before sliding the card across the glass counter. For a second, I wasn't breathing. What if the payment doesn't go through? What if this moment—the one that felt like reclaiming something sacred—was about to turn into humiliation?

The woman behind the counter took it without blinking, swiped it smoothly, and smiled as she handed it back.

Approved.

Relief flushed through my whole body, but I tried to play it cool— smiling politely, tucking the receipt into my bag like this was something I did all the time. Like this wasn't the most I'd ever spent on myself for something that didn't have a practical use. I stepped into the sunlight, floating on air, a quiet smile on my lips and the unshakable knowing that I was the richest woman in the world. Not because of what I had, but because of who I had become. There was no regret—only power.

Back at the van, the women were buzzing with energy. Shopping bags rustled, and laughter bubbled up from the group like champagne. I slid into a seat just before Lilly boarded, her white linen dress glowing in the amber light.

"Okay, ladies," she said. "I see a lot of smiles on everyone's faces. I would love to know, what did you learn about yourself from this experience?"

There was a beat of silence, then Sofia spoke first. "That I've really been afraid to say yes to myself."

Mikayla followed, her tone lighter than it had been all day. "I learned I don't need to buy anything to be worthy, so I broke the rules. I looked around but didn't buy a single, solitary thing." There was an audible gasp from a few of the women. "But don't worry, Lilly. The exercise was a success because I feel more worthy from not buying something than I ever did by buying something."

Lilly smiled a genuine smile, and her laughter rang out, bright and clear. "I think this is a first for me, congratulating someone on not completing the assignment. As you all know her story, you can appreciate how powerful it is that she chose herself by saying yes to her authentic desire and no to a purchase, especially knowing she would have to face me at the end of the day. Thank you, Mikayla, for honoring yourself in such a valuable way; your decision speaks volumes about your evolving relationship with money—and with yourself."

A round of applause erupted, making Mikayla smile, then blush as the warmth spread through her cheeks.

Once things quieted again, Lilly asked, "Anyone else have anything to share?"

I didn't overthink it. I just let the words fall. "I learned…" I paused, touching the ring lightly with my thumb. "That I am worthy. No matter what, I am worthy."

Heads nodded, and the air vibrated with the soft, shared sigh of agreement, like they had learned that too.

One by one, the women shared their experiences, and we all supported each other. Then the van pulled up to a private stretch of beach just as the sky dipped into lavender. I stepped down and gasped. Lilly had outdone herself.

A wide white pergola stood in the sand, draped in soft muslin and dotted with strings of warm, twinkling lights that flickered like fireflies. Beneath it were rattan chairs, each with bright floral cushions and matching napkins in bold, happy prints. A long table was set with candles in glass jars and bowls overflowing with tropical blooms. And just beyond, a server stood waiting with a silver tray full of pink drinks in oversized flutes, each crowned with a yellow flower.

I accepted my drink with a smile so wide and genuine, it felt like it reached all the way through me, warming me from the inside out. I chose a seat beside a woman named Lori, who had an elegant, earthy vibe. Her dress was cotton and flowy, her hair in soft waves streaked with sun. As we sat, she leaned in.

"How was your shopping trip?" she asked.

I held up my hand.

She gasped. "Oh wow, that is gorgeous."

"I wasn't going to buy anything," I admitted. "And then… I found this. Or maybe it found me."

She nodded. "Sometimes the thing we were meant to have shows up when we stop looking for it."

"I feel like that's exactly what happened," I nodded back. "I'm still not sure how I'm going to pay it off, but I love this so much I'm more than happy to figure it out."

Dinner was coconut rice and crispy fried duck—something the chef called a Bali specialty. It was salty and rich and paired per-fectly with the sweet punch in our glasses. The food, the laughter, the glow of the lanterns—it all felt like the kind of night you re-member forever.

And then, as plates were cleared, Lilly stood again.

"One last invitation for the evening," she said. "Around the cove, you'll find a chair for each of you facing the ocean. They're spaced apart to give you privacy. I invite you to take your journal and just... be with your truth. What came up today? What softened? What surprised you?"

I walked along the shore until I came across a red chair with a yellow and white striped pillow. Sitting cross-legged on the chair, my journal on my lap, I looked over the water and listened to the waves lapping the shore. The sky was like a watercolor painting, glowing with warm hues of amber, peach, and rose gold, fading upward into muted lavenders, dusty blues, and deepening indigo. The light was gentle—an in-between moment where day exhales and night inhales.

My fingers traced the outline of my ring. I had never spent that much money on something so seemingly impractical. Not for me. It had always been about the needs of my ex, the kids, or the house, never about my *wants*. Unless there was wine involved. And sadness. And a sale.

But today... today was different.

I opened up my journal and began scribbling across the page.

Today, I chose myself. Today, I became the kind of woman who doesn't wait for permission, who doesn't ask for a sale. Today, I remembered I am allowed to want whatever sets my soul on fire. That I can wear it, carry it, and become it. I am worthy. I am free. I choose me.

I closed my eyes, the tension leaving my body with a long, slow exhale. A wave of contentment washed over me in rhythm with the ocean.

My phone buzzed beside me, and I jumped a little at the sound. I picked it up, expecting a message from Chloe or maybe a group text from the retreat.

It was an email from my lawyer.

Subject: Refund initiated—Overpayment on file

I blinked.

The amount of the overpayment was *exactly* the cost of the ring. A laugh escaped my throat, half in joy, half in disbelief.

Kismet. Of course. The universe wasn't just nodding in approval. It was *celebrating* with me.

I closed my eyes and let the tears flow. Not from sadness, but from knowing. I wasn't just healing. I was reclaiming myself and stepping into the life I was meant to live.

The ring on my finger shimmered again.

And I realized that this was the kind of wealth I came here for.

***

Learn how to create your own luxury shopping experience.
Find out how on page 205.

Chapter 9

Vision of Prosperity

Lori

I sauntered towards the pool, the early sun warm on my shoulders as the birds chirped their morning song. The silk floral cover-up, cool and smooth against my skin, awakened a forgotten sense of pleasure as it brushed against my thigh. The emerald green bathing suit, soft and luxurious against my skin, clung to my curves in all the right places. When I tried them both on at the boutique yesterday, the bright lights and the mirror reflected a version of myself I hadn't seen in a long time: The person I was before becoming lost in marriage, motherhood and a successful career in marketing.

With each step, a forgotten boldness returned, a rhythm of rediscovery. Deep inside, beneath the familiar ache of self-doubt and the weight of years spent shrinking from life, I felt a jolt—a pulse of something electric, like a sudden spark igniting in the darkness. And I felt sexy. It wasn't about getting noticed or looking for approval. It was just because I am. And I let myself feel it.

During yesterday's workshop, Lilly's words struck a chord, revealing how I'd been accepting *that's just what happens after 29 years of marriage* as my reality, hindering my financial goals. I bought into the idea that my life isn't about me any longer, and there isn't any room to think about what I want.

It started one morning five years ago when my husband, Joe, filled with nervous excitement, finally opened the doors to the business he had talked about since I met him. I was so proud of him pursuing his dreams that I happily let him manage our family finances—a tremendous weight off my shoulders. My day was already filled with a whirlwind of multitasking madness; a symphony of children's needs, preparing food, and the constant mental buzz of an overwhelming to-do list, all on top of my responsibilities as a VP at work. I was grateful for the help.

About a year ago, I logged into our online banking and noticed our savings account was empty, a shocking zero staring back at me. He explained it was a temporary setback, a short-term need to boost the bottom line of his business. Preoccupied with a million other things, I let it go. Weeks passed, and then one morning, I found an overdue bill for our credit line. My worries escalated, and I shared my concerns with Joe. That conversation turned into our first serious fight, and the silence, heavy with unspoken hurt and anger, lasted for days.

From there, the constant drain on our finances filled me with frustration and anger, and our repeated arguments about his business were explosive. They all ended with his sharp, accusatory words, "Don't you trust me? I can handle it. I've got this." Who was I to tear down his dream? I'm his wife—isn't supporting him what I'm supposed to do? I tried. But when I heard I was getting a bonus, I opened up a secret account of my own and deposited it there. If I hadn't, I wouldn't be here in Bali.

I was a dedicated saver, a habit I developed long before I ever met Joe. As a matter of fact, the money I saved was the only reason we could afford our first house. But now I feel like everything I've tried to save slips away like water through a sieve, drained by his spending. And I don't know how to stop it.

The last words he said to me as I walked out the door were, "If you go, don't come back."

Since then, he has not responded to any of my messages.

I dropped my beach bag onto the cushioned lounge chair and gazed out at the calm ocean over the edge of the infinity pool. The surface of the pool mirrored the sky, cool and still in the soft morning light. The water shimmered in deep, tranquil blues, blurring the almost indistinct line between pool and ocean. It was calling me to join in the calm, a place to slip in and let go of all my worries.

I dove deep under the water, feeling the cool embrace of the depths and hearing the muffled sounds of the world above. Surfacing, a strange sense of peace settled over me as I realized I had chosen this. I finally chose myself.

I flipped onto my back, arms flung wide, and the sensation of weightlessness made me feel like an angel drifting in the gentle breeze. As I took a deep breath, the heavy burden of my husband's anger and my family's expectations lifted, leaving me feeling like I could float all day. There was a lightness in my chest now, a quiet confidence that everything would work out.

Yesterday's wealthy self-image exercise had me journaling about my ideal self. In my life, I juggled the responsibilities of being a mother, a wife, a VP, a daughter, and a sister. I'm a caretaker at heart, always striving to ensure everyone around me feels content and looked after. After that list, my mind went completely blank.

With Lilly's gentle guidance and insightful questions, I realized I hadn't been accurate in my answer. I was listing my roles—mother, wife, and executive—instead of describing the person underneath, the person I was before I became any of these things. Here I am a day later, still wrestling with these questions.

Who am I? Who do I want to be?

***

After showering and getting dressed, I made my way over to the pavilion. When I entered, there was a gentle rustle of mats and a soft thud of pillows settling as the others prepared for the session to begin. The air felt different, quieter, heavier. The space felt hushed and expectant, as if awaiting something sacred.

I walked over to my table, clutching a worn leather binder close to my chest. I'd looked at it a million times, and the well-worn edges, frayed corners, and dog-eared pages felt familiar beneath my fingertips. It wasn't just a binder. It was everything I hadn't dared to speak aloud: A collection of secret dreams and desires. I dropped the book with a soft thud onto the wooden table and headed to collect my mat and cushion.

Calm and grounded, as always, Lilly entered the space, the quiet hum of the room settling around her like a comforting blanket. She was wearing a black fitted catsuit and a white silk kimono with hand-painted cherry blossoms on it. I sighed. I wished I were always as inspired and uplifted as when I looked at Lilly.

"Good morning. What a great day we had yesterday, and I am really looking forward to today. On the agenda today is our visioning workshop," Lilly began. "Before we dive in, let's take a few minutes for a breathwork exercise, focusing on the rhythm of our breath and the sensations in our bodies. Incorporating daily morning breathwork into my life over a decade ago has been transformative; the conscious control of my breath has helped me navigate some of life's most challenging moments with resilience and inner peace. So, I have asked Katie to come back today and start our day connecting with our breath."

Lilly took her seat on her cushion to the left, and Katie stood at the front of the room.

"Thank you, Lilly. Ladies, let's drop into our bodies," Katie said. "Close your eyes and bring your hands to your heart. Bring your awareness to your heart. Feel your heartbeat. And notice your breath."

I took a deep breath in and let out a short exhale.

"Breathe in now for four counts and out for four counts."

A tightening sensation constricted my chest, and I struggled to take a full breath. The pressure crept up my throat, making it hard to swallow.

Breathing with awareness was more challenging than expected. I couldn't seem to settle in and breathe freely.

"Inhale, one, two, three, four, and hold." She paused. "Now exhale one, two, three, four... Ahhhhhhhhhhh... And again."

With each inhale and exhale, I felt my belly rise and fall, and slowly, a shared rhythm developed between us, a comforting connection. My mind wandered back to this morning's swim in the pool and the feeling of layers of my old self melting away. Then my mother's voice came into my mind. *Your job as a woman is to ensure everyone has a good meal, a beautiful, clean home, and to be a supportive wife and mother.* Where was *me* in all of that?

Katie's voice, soft as a feather, brought me back to the floor. "We are regulating the nervous system," she said, her tone hushed and reassuring. "Allowing spaciousness in the body, so you feel a release of tension and these deep breaths expand your chest, open the door for wisdom to flow in. We're doing this because women so often disconnect from their bodies, living in their heads instead of their hearts. Life rushes by, and we barely register the cool air filling our lungs, the subtle exhale, the unnoticed dance of breathing. We exist without true awareness within our own beings."

Katie's heartfelt words struck a chord, resonating deeply within me. I've been walking through life, holding my breath, with my mind in overdrive. My superpower is reading a room, sensing the unspoken needs and thoughts of others, anticipating their desires before they articulate them, and adjusting my behavior accordingly. But what about me? My desires?

I stored those neatly away in the quiet darkness of my desk drawer, tucked safely within my binder's protection.

"Keep taking deep breaths, in and out. Release all the tension on the exhale. Let it all out," Katie continued. "Now, I want you to give yourself a big hug on the next exhale and whisper sweet nothings into your own heart. I love ending breathwork with a personal love letter."

Katie took a step back, and Lilly stood up with her palms together over her heart with a small bow. "Thank you, Katie. This is always such an amazing experience tapping into breath. It's like a wave of calmness washes over me. Your sessions never disappoint."

Lilly stepped over and hugged Katie. Then she turned to us as Katie headed for the door. "Please put away your cushions and mats and return to your tables so we can begin today's lesson," Lilly instructed. She paused, smiling. "Wow, did that sound a little like a kindergarten teacher? I always wanted to be a teacher," Lilly laughed, the sound echoing through the group as we all joined in.

With quiet patience, Lilly watched as each of us carefully stacked our cushions and mats by the wall before returning to our own desks. A soft rustle of fabric and paper filled the air as each woman placed her water bottle on her table and pulled her journal and pen from her bag. When everyone finally settled in their seats, Lilly cleared her throat and began.

"Now let's revisit *her*... the version of you we met yesterday, your wealthy self-image. If you had a magic wand, what would your life look like with her leading the way?"

"Close your eyes and imagine that what you want to accomplish has come true, and everyone is celebrating you. What are you wearing? Where are you? Who are you with? This is a celebration of you, so you get to choose. Notice who is there with you during this celebration. What does it feel like? I want you to create a movie in your mind that captures everything you want."

I struggled for a moment, my mind a blank canvas, trying to pull an image into focus.

Then, the tears came.

Because I knew *her*. I had played this story out in my mind so many times that the images were almost as real as life. Every morning before anyone else arrived at the office, I sat at my desk, building *her,* page by page, dream by dream.

She was the vibrant, radiant me. She walked barefoot in the sand, laughing with two beautiful children, arms open to life. This version of me boldly spoke her truth at work and at home. She built a successful marketing firm, boasting a team of incredibly talented and innovative creatives. The world celebrated this Lori for her support of groundbreaking products that make a positive impact, improving lives globally. She had complete financial freedom; she could go anywhere, do anything, and be with anyone she pleased, without a single worry about money.

Lilly continued, "This is the happiest you have ever been. The healthiest and wealthiest you have ever felt. Notice your expression at this moment. The smile, the joy, the love, and the peace. You are so proud of yourself; it came together exactly how you wanted it and even better. You are achieving everything you set out to do. Stay in this feeling of having achieved that success and be grateful for it all." Lilly walked behind us as she continued to speak. "Ladies, here is the truth: You always knew you were meant for more. You knew it, and that is why you are here. Sometimes your future self just needs a witness. Someone to say: I see you. I believe in you. I've been you."

Tears streamed down my face. That version of myself seemed so perfect, so unattainable, that the desire to be her felt like a physical need. I envied her carefree spirit and wished I could be her right now. I craved that feeling of effortless ease, the deep, calming peace, and the strong sense of purpose she enjoyed. In her, I saw a life filled with the things I craved—financial security, strong bonds with loved ones, and a deep sense of self-worth that was missing from my life.

"Lori," Lilly said, stepping closer to me. "This seems to have resonated with you on a deep level. Would you like to share what you imagined for the future version of you?"

I didn't even remember standing up—only that suddenly my heart was hammering in my ears, my binder trembling in my hands. "I... I brought something," I said, my voice thin. "I've never shown anyone this."

I grabbed the binder that was on my table. "I started this a year ago," I said. "Right when my husband, Joe, started spiraling. His business was falling apart, but he wouldn't stop. He drained everything. I supported his vision, but I buried my own in this binder."

A photo slipped out as I opened it—women snorkeling in turquoise waters, faces turned to the sun.

"I saw this exact photo on Lilly's ad," I said, my voice trembling. "It was one I had torn out of a magazine a year ago. As soon as I saw it, I knew I had to come."

Lilly stepped closer, her expression unreadable for a moment, and then she smiled. "That photo..." she said slowly, "was taken right here, on this beach. It is the reason my husband and I vacationed here, and once I saw all of this in person, I knew this was the place I wanted to do my first retreat."

Gasps fluttered around the room.

"You carried that image in your binder," Lilly continued, "and now you are standing in it. That is the power of visualization. That is the power of becoming energetically aligned with what you desire—even when you don't know how it will come to you."

I stared at the photo in my hands, stunned. The exact same shore. The same shade of sky. The same joy on their faces.

My voice cracked. Clearing my throat, I continued. "I secretly set aside money for this trip from a work bonus. When Joe found out, he was furious." I looked around the circle. "But I have had enough of doing everything for everyone but me."

Lilly stepped forward, her gaze soft. "Is there anything else you've manifested from your dream binder?"

The pages rustled softly as I turned them, each magazine photo a glimpse into the dreams I held dear.

"Yes, I make over $100,000 annually, so I can check that off my list. Wow... in just one year, my salary jumped from $75,000 to $100,000. The fact that this was a goal of mine hadn't even registered in my mind until now."

With a flick of my wrist, I flipped the page, a thrill of anticipation building as I looked to see what else I had accomplished off my list. "And I completed a sprint triathlon in April. I sucked, but I was proud of myself for finishing it. And look at this," I exclaimed, gesturing towards the model who stood poised in a breathtaking high-end evening gown. "This dress is so much like the one I wore to my work gala in January. I've been going through this book for over a year, and I haven't even processed the fact that I have achieved some of it already."

Lilly looked at me, smiling. "And who is the woman you are becoming by completing the dreams you have so beautifully captured in the binder?"

I exhaled, feeling the truth rise like a tide.

"She's brave. Magnetic. Morning brings excitement instead of the usual apprehension. She starts the day with a happy heart. Wherever she is, at a beach with her children or an amazing resort like this, she doesn't cover herself up or hide in a bathing suit because she is proud of the body that has carried her through every season of life. She lets herself be seen and heard without caring what others think. And, she keeps control over her own money and decides how it will be used, including giving to the charities she loves. She travels around the globe without fear or concern." A newfound confidence radiated out of me. "I will not apologize for dreaming anymore," I declared.

Lilly nodded gently. "This is beautiful, Lori. Now tell me, how does it feel?"

I closed my eyes again.

"It feels amazing. It's like a tiger is growing inside of me, powerful and unafraid, giving me the confidence to chase my dreams."

I thought about all the photos in the binder. Something shifted. "Bring it on! I am ready and excited to see whatever comes next."

I opened my eyes to find the women leaning in, some with tears streaming freely. I wasn't alone.

Lilly placed her hand on my binder. "This," she said, "isn't just a collection of dreams. It's a contract with your higher self. You are *her*. When you live from that vision, your energy shifts. Your choices change. And the Universe responds. So when you go home, do not ask for permission. Imagine your life every day, see it clearly and feel all the feelings that go with that glorious life, and then look for alignment in your reality. It's not a matter of whether you can accomplish what you dream of—because you can. The deeper question is: does it align with the life you want to create?"

"But what about Joe and my children? Isn't it selfish to spend all of this time making myself better or to follow my dreams? What if becoming *her* means leaving our marriage? And how can I attract more good into my life when I feel such a low vibe at home? I struggle with choosing for myself. I mean, I love my new bathing suit and cover-up, but it took me hours of internal debate and anxiety before I finally made the purchase. Afterwards, all I could think of was what Joe would say about spending money on frivolous things," I sighed and shook my head. "Part of me is happy that I've already accomplished some of my goals, but part of me thinks I will never be *her* if I'm with Joe."

"I think it is time to have the queen conversation," Lilly said. "And I'm going to need to sit down for this one."

***

Now it's your turn to begin creating a visual reminder of your financial purpose. The steps are found on page 207.

Chapter 10

Harnessing Your Queen Energy

Lilly

I sat on the edge of my chair with my bare feet grounding me on the cool, smooth wooden floor of the pavilion. Gazing at the semicircle before me, I saw eight women, each with a unique and compelling life story to tell, yet bound by a shared, quiet ache: A longing to remember who they were before life asked them to forget.

I took a deep breath and exhaled slowly, calling in the words that would connect with these women.

"So, let's talk about queen energy."

A few eyebrows lifted slightly, hinting at curiosity; a few smiles bloomed, warm and welcoming. It didn't come as a surprise to me. The idea always lands a little alien at first, especially if you've been raised to believe that being a loving person equates to serving others, even if it is detrimental to yourself.

I continued, "I wasn't always this version of me. I used to be a servant in my own life. Not a queen. No, definitely not royalty. I was the one picking up the pieces, making excuses for a man who didn't love me well, constantly trying to keep the peace while quietly dying inside."

I let the words settle, watching the resonance ripple across their faces.

"My first marriage was full of disrespect, dishonor, and emotional abandonment. I had no self-respect. And guess what? No one else respected me either. Not truly. Because our self-worth sets the bar for how others treat us. If you don't like your relationship, stop trying to change the other person. Work on you. Build your confidence. Raise your standards. Then, those who are meant to rise with you will. And those who aren't... will fall away."

There were slow nods. I saw Lori shift slightly in her seat.

"I hit rock bottom when I got caught shoplifting. I was poor, broken, and left behind. My husband had walked away. And I realized there was no one left to change but me."

I stepped closer to the group, my hand resting over my heart. "Queen energy was foreign to me then. I spent weeks researching the concept, and I became obsessed. Now I know a queen isn't just a woman with a crown—she's the one who takes her commitments to herself seriously. She leads her life with integrity. She doesn't wait to be chosen. She chooses herself."

I paused to let the weight of that land.

"And that's exactly what I did. I painstakingly rebuilt myself from the ground up. The first time I said no, I felt a profound sense of self-worth, a newfound confidence in my ability to set boundaries. There's a quiet strength, a liberating power in the simple act of saying no. I stopped apologizing for my dreams and refused to let anyone silence them. I stopped the pathetic begging and, instead, I started expecting the world to bring me all I wanted. It didn't happen overnight. It took years—years of crying on the floor, whispering affirmations I didn't yet believe, barely recognizing my reflection, while trying to visualize the woman I longed to be."

I walked over to Lori and bent down to her eye level.

"And when I finally felt whole again—when I knew in my bones that I was enough—I met my second husband." I touched her arm. "This time, I didn't lower my vibe. I didn't shrink or soften to fit someone else's comfort. He rose to meet me. And he has continued to rise, side by side with me, for the past ten years. We lead together. Not perfectly, but powerfully. That's the difference. That's the gift of queen energy—it calls in the match, not the fixer."

I stood up and took a step back from Lori's table.

"And today, I want to talk about how this applies to you, Lori—because I see your story reflected in so many of the women I meet."

Lori looked up at me, her expression a mix of vulnerability and strength.

"You're confident in your career," I said. "You're a powerhouse. You're a VP, a go-getter, a woman people trust to lead."

Lori nodded slightly, her shoulders tightening.

"But at home, your confidence gets dimmed. For five years, you've been shrinking yourself in that relationship. And somewhere along the way, you started believing that smaller was safer. You don't feel good enough in your own house. Not with him. Not even with your kids."

The other women listened with silent reverence.

"You've worked. You've mothered. You've grocery-shopped, scheduled, cleaned, planned, and made sure everyone else was taken care of. You made life smooth for everyone else. Meanwhile, your needs and your joy were rationed."

Lori's throat worked to swallow something hard. Her hands gripped her thighs.

"I want you to hear this: You were taught that being a good wife meant being a servant. But that model is broken. A queen doesn't serve her king—she stands beside him with great expectation for both of them. And if he can't rise to meet her? She rises anyway."

I stepped closer, putting my hand on her table. "Lori, it seems that during the past five years, you've forgotten your own frequency. But now... you are remembering."

Lori's eyes shimmered as tears pooled at the edges.

"A queen sets the tone. She leads herself. She doesn't need approval to act. She trusts her knowing. She protects her peace. And she does not apologize for her desires. Do you want to step into your queen energy? Start with this very simple question: What would a queen do?"

I glanced around the room and felt the shift before I even saw it. Shoulders drew back, spines straightened, and a new kind of presence settled over the women. I watched, awed, as they each seemed to rise—not from their seats, but from within themselves. The energy of the queen was no longer just an idea—it was alive, and they were inhaling it like oxygen.

I turned back to Lori. "And you, my love, are stepping back into your rightful place. You're beginning to use your voice again. You're seeing that what you tolerated in your life for so long isn't normal—it isn't love."

Lori wiped a tear, then nodded.

"You don't need to fix him," I said softly. "You need to find *you*. And the more power you build within yourself, the more clarity you will have. Then, you will know exactly what to do."

I took a final breath and looked around at all of them.

"Remember this: a queen takes her commitments to herself seriously. She knows what she wants and does not let anyone else talk her out of it. A queen walks through fear because she knows something beautiful lives on the other side. And a king? A real king does not wish for her to diminish her light. He encourages it and matches it. He makes space for her to lead—and leads alongside her with strength, love, and honor."

I walked to the front of the room. With both hands outstretched, I said, "Today is your invitation. It is time to pick up your crown."

***

Go to page 209 to learn more about how to harness your queen energy.

Chapter 11

Lifetime Habits of Prosperity

Roxanne

You're late again, Roxanne, I muttered under my breath, the ice in my latte clinking softly as I adjusted the sweating container in my hand. *Why are you always late?* I asked myself, not expecting an answer, just hearing the familiar beat of disappointment tapping in my chest. But then I smirked. *Who cares if I'm late?* I'm sure I won't be the last one back from lunch.

I flicked my long, black hair and smiled, adding a little swag to my step. I have never cared what people think. I don't do performances. I don't do boxes. I love that I am bold, stubborn, and untamed, and I'm being my true Aries self. I know deep down, there is no one else like me: Carefree. The wild one. The woman who gets to do whatever she wants, every day of her life.

As I passed the full-length mirror stationed just outside the washrooms in the pavilion, my reflection caught me off guard. My lightly glossed lips curled into a slow, satisfied smile as I took in the blue-and-white Dolce & Gabbana silk dress that I bought in Rome on a high of adrenaline after closing the biggest client project of my career. The femininity of the dress was offset by the trail of tattoos that curled up from the top of my foot to my thigh, a constellation of symbols and coordinates, half-hidden by the long, flowing skirt. Each one marked a chapter of my journey.

My green eyes sparkled from the light sconces on either side of the mirror, and my skin glowed. All of the Botox, fillers, and facials were worth this reflection. *Damn, she's something*, I thought, actually admiring my own reflection.

But then there was a twist in my stomach. Not hunger. Not nerves. Something else. A slow build of dread. Because in just a couple of minutes, I'll be stuck in a circle of strangers, sipping herbal tea and talking about feelings. I exhaled long and slow.

What the hell am I doing here?

Yesterday's workshop about discovering your wealthy self-image only confirmed what I already knew: I am her. I am living that life now. I built a thriving graphic design business, one that lets me work from anywhere, and I've turned the world into my personal playground. Every new country I land in, I find the rhythm of the streets, the pulse of the parties, and people who are drawn to my light like moths to a flame. I've never been afraid to travel alone. I wear my confidence like a second skin. It's my gift. It's what makes me magnetic.

My parents... well, they had other dreams for me. They wanted me to have small-town stability with a nine-to-five job and a good pension, find the perfect husband, and have babies. Their dreams for their children were shaped by survival. They fled a war-torn country with two suitcases and terrified eyes. Canada was their chance to live a better life. Their mission was peace, safety, and a future for us. They never wanted us to feel the hunger or fear they had known.

I can still hear my father's voice: *Money doesn't grow on trees, Roxanne. You have to work hard for it. You've got champagne taste and no savings account.* My mom would sigh as she folded laundry and eyed my latest purchases.

They were scared, always. To them, money was tied directly to personal safety. You saved it, hoarded it, protected it. You didn't enjoy it—you preserved it, just in case the world collapsed again. But even as a little girl, I knew I wasn't wired like them. They counted pennies, and I chased dreams. Where they reused foil and saved elastic bands, I bought the latest fashion.

For the past few days, I'd been second-guessing why I booked this retreat. Don't get me wrong, I love Bali. The food, the people, the air that smells like frangipani and incense. But this? A circle of women journaling their way to transformation? I don't know what I was expecting... but it wasn't *this*.

Their energy was quiet, reserved, and soft, and mine was more tequila at sunset and dancing on tables. I felt like the wild card tossed into a deck of women with gratitude journals, linen pants, and crystals tucked in their bras. I had booked this retreat on a whim, classic Roxanne style. Chasing a quick fix.

Sure, I've got debt. Who doesn't? I make great money. I live on my terms. That matters. Freedom is my currency. And if you had scrolled through my Instagram last month, I was sipping cocktails in Mykonos, my skin glowing in golden hour, and you wouldn't think I needed a damn thing.

"Good afternoon, ladies." I could hear Lilly's voice echoing into the hallway. "Welcome back to the afternoon portion of Day Three,"

Just before I stepped into the room, my phone buzzed.

Payment declined.

My stomach tightened. I quickly flipped the phone face down, cheeks flushing even though no one was watching.

Again? I whispered, barely audible. I was halfway around the world, surrounded by paradise, and I still couldn't outrun the chaos. Maybe I did need to be here.

When I entered the room, I caught Lilly mid-sentence. She looked up at me with a soft and cheerful smile, motioning her hand for me to join in. "Hi Roxanne, thank you for joining us." I felt a flush of heat come across my face, filled with embarrassment. So much for not caring about what people thought of me being late.

She waited until I found my seat.

"Before the break," Lilly continued, "I encouraged you to reflect on the vision tied to your financial purpose. If you remember from Day One, we explored how your thoughts create feelings, and those feelings drive your actions. Today, we move into action." She paused, letting the words settle.

"Your actions are made up of habits. Habits create behaviors. Behaviors create patterns you often don't even notice because they're automatic. But if you want a life that matches your purpose, your actions have to be aligned and intentional."

A slow sigh escaped me. *Perfect. Another reminder I didn't do the homework*, I thought.

During the lunch break, while the others were sprawled out under palm trees journaling about their future selves, I was poolside with a cocktail in hand, sunglasses on, tan deepening, pretending this was just another luxurious Wednesday. But the truth? While my body was in Bali, my heart was somewhere else entirely.

Mykonos. That's where I met him: Carter. *The one.* He was backpacking through the Greek islands. He was tall, tanned, had gorgeous, messy golden hair, and looked like he belonged on the front cover of a travel magazine. Somehow, this amazing man chose to sit beside me at the bar.

We talked for hours that night. Laughed like old friends. Kissed like we were rewriting the stars. It wasn't just chemistry—it was something more. He made me feel grounded and wild at the same time. Safe and free. And now? He's back in Australia. He invited me to visit him in Sydney, and I'm already mapping it out, the flights, the dates, and the outfits.

But lately, something's been gnawing at me. What will he think when he finds out that I'm drowning in debt and creditors are after me? That I've built a beautiful life online, but it's crumbling behind the screen?

And for the first time... I actually *want* to change. I want to be the kind of woman a man like *that* could build a life with. I just don't know how to become her. It feels like I'm too far gone and there's no point of return.

Lilly's soft yet mesmerizing voice brought me back to the present.

"I want to open up our discussion with this question: What is one habit you know is holding you back, but you still defend or deny?"

I gasped—too loud. Every head turned. My stomach dropped as I forced a smile and shook my head, trying to laugh it off. Inside, though, something cracked.

"Roxanne?" Lilly's voice floated gently toward me. "Is there something you'd like to share?"

The word *deny* was beating in my head like a war drum. Deny. Deny. Deny.

Right then—buzz. My phone again. Another vibration. Probably another message from the credit card company. It wasn't loud, but it hit like a taser. It was a divine shove to reveal the truth.

I looked up. My throat tightened. "I owe..." I began, the words barely audible. "I owe a lot of people money." The air in the room shifted. I could see the women leaning in. Some blinked. Others tilted their heads like they weren't sure they heard me right.

"Creditors contact me every day. My phone doesn't stop buzzing. I've been swiping my card and booking flights like the money would magically appear. I convinced myself that as long as my life looked good on Instagram, the rest would fall into place. But the truth? I don't have my shit together. Not even close."

I paused and took a breath, trying to hold back the tears.

"My parents always budgeted everything. I swore I'd never be like them. Budget life isn't my vibe. But this... mess? It's not working either. I want to break the habit of overspending."

Lilly's eyes softened. She walked slowly toward me. "That was incredibly brave, Roxanne. And powerful. When we stop resisting the truth, we begin to *see* clearly and become aware of our actions. And by the way, I've been where you are."

Wait—what?

"When my business finally took off, the money poured in and it poured right out," Lilly said with a soft laugh. "Money was like water slipping through my fingers. Designer heels. Luxurious spa treatments. Business-class upgrades. Lavish dinners with people I barely even liked."

Her voice dipped. "I told myself I was celebrating. That I deserved it because I had gone without for so long. But the truth was... I tried to quiet the ache of not-enoughness with things I once only dreamed of."

The room fell silent.

"Abundance," Lilly said, her voice low but steady, "is not about how much flows in—it's about how much you're willing to hold emotionally, energetically and financially. It is about being aligned with your vision for yourself and feeling grounded in your habits that create peace, not panic. It is not a number; it is a feeling."

She paused, letting the silence stretch just enough for that idea to land.

She turned towards me, with her hand over her heart. "To have a prosperous life is not just about how much money you make or spend. It's a way of life balancing what you want with the income you have. That takes a combination of discipline and clarity to create the life you want, one intention at a time."

Lilly walked back to the front of the room.

"Let's all take a few minutes to journal on that same question again. This time, observe your habits like a scientist. No judgment. No shame. Just clarity. The habits you find are not good or bad—they are either aligned or they are blocking you from becoming your best self."

I opened my journal and wrote.

What habits are keeping me stuck?

I thought about Carter, the Australian man I'm falling in love with and how grounded he seemed. I want a real future with someone like him. What was stopping me?

And just like that, the truth spilled out:

Wake up late –> Skip breakfast –> Miss paying invoices –> Buy lunch out –> Scroll Instagram –> FOMO –> Impulse shopping –> NSFs –> Shame –> Avoidance –> More spending –> More running –> More pretending –> Repeat.

It was a loop. One habit crashing into the next and then back again to the beginning. I felt a wave of overwhelm rise up. *How do you even begin to undo this?*

I closed my eyes. Took a deep breath. *You can do this, Roxanne. You have to do this. You can't keep living like this. What steps do you need to take to seriously consider a relationship with Carter?*

Lilly looked up from her seat like she could feel the shift in the air.

"Are any of you stuck?"

Several of us raised our hands.

She walked to the whiteboard. Her energy had changed. She was focused. Clear. "What if I told you that you don't have to overhaul your entire life to change it?" she said. "You just need one small habit—*a domino habit*—to start the shift."

She picked up a marker and, with deliberate strokes, wrote in big, clean letters:

Domino Habit
One intentional act that knocks down the rest.

"It's not about having it all figured out by 8 a.m.," she said. "What matters is choosing one habit, one small anchor that supports the life you are creating. Whether that moment happens at sunrise, midday, or right before bed, it still counts. Any habit, at any time, can become a catalyst for transformation."

Then she added below it:

Habit Stacking
Pairing a new habit with something you already do or want to do.

That part made my ears perk up. This wasn't about blowing up my life. It wasn't about becoming some hyper-organized, color-coded finance goddess overnight.

It was just about starting with one habit and then pairing it with something I already did or wanted to do, which sounded... possible. I swallowed, then raised my hand before I could talk myself out of it.

"Lilly... would you be willing to help me figure out how to shift this?" I asked, my voice louder than I expected. "I think it's finally time I get my shit together. I need to make some real changes."

Lilly turned to me with that grounded, gentle energy she always carried—like nothing could shake her.

"Absolutely," she said. "That's exactly why we are here. Would you feel comfortable sharing a few of the habits you'd like to shift?"

My stomach flipped. I wasn't ready to *say* them *out loud*—not all of them. But my life won't change until I figure out how to take control of it.

"I wake up late. I avoid checking my accounts. I eat out every day. I tell myself I'll deal with it later, but later never comes. I shop to feel better and then ignore the guilt. I've never filed my taxes on time. I swipe my card and cross my fingers." I laughed nervously, trying to make it sound lighter than it felt. "Honestly, I don't even know where half my money goes... I just know it's *not* going where it should."

"Roxanne," Lilly said softly, tilting her head just slightly. "Is there one habit you can think of implementing while you are here that could be your first domino?"

I didn't even pause.

"Wake up early," I blurted out, louder than I meant to. "I just said to myself before walking into the pavilion that I'm always late. So..."

My words trailed off, caught midair as the weight of what I had just declared sank in. The truth of it settled heavily on my chest. Saying it out loud meant I had to do it, and that scared me more than I wanted to admit. I looked down, fidgeting with the edge of the cushion beneath me, suddenly very aware of how grounded everyone else seemed.

"I love that my life is different every day," I continued, my voice quieter now, almost confessional. "That unpredictability... It makes me feel like I am living an adventure. Structure? Routines? That just makes me feel like I am stuck in some loop. Like life would get... boring."

Heat crept up my neck. I wasn't used to this kind of exposure. Then, I felt it. A gentle squeeze on my arm. Mikayla had leaned over, and her hand lingered for just a second, long enough to say *I get it* without a single word spoken. I glanced at her. She nodded, eyes soft, understanding—the kind of support I didn't even know I needed.

Lilly stepped closer, her presence calm and grounding. "That's a powerful insight, Roxanne," she said. "Life doesn't have to be boring for you to be in control. Good habits can be woven into even the most adventurous days. Does your morning skincare routine change if you are in a different country?"

I laughed. "Of course not."

"And that is why you have such beautiful skin. Consistent repetition is how to build what you want. So, start with a wake-up time that feels realistic for you, something you can stick to and build momentum." She smiled gently. "Can you think of another habit you would consider stacking on to an early wake-up time?"

I hesitated, pressing my lips together. A dozen ideas ran through my head, all of them half-baked. But then something clicked. "Well," I said, "I think I'd like to start meditating." It came out before I could second-guess it. "When we did that session with Katie, I don't know... I felt calm. Like, actually calm for the entire day. I couldn't tell you the last time I felt that quiet on the inside."

Lilly lit up like I'd handed her a love letter. "That's a beautiful awareness, Roxanne," she said, beaming. "That is how we build a Prosperity Habit Stack: One intentional step at a time." She placed her palms together at her heart and nodded, like something sacred had just taken root.

I sat with it for a moment, that image of starting my day on purpose instead of default. Waking up early. Meditating. Being with myself instead of running from myself. And then, out of nowhere, something I'd seen weeks ago bubbled up.

"You know..." I said slowly, "I remember seeing one of your Instagram posts about something called a 'money date.' At the time, I scrolled past it. I wasn't ready to hear it, I guess." I paused, chewing the inside of my cheek. "But now, I think I want to know. Like, really know—what does that actually look like?"

Lilly smiled, her eyes lighting up. "Yes, I talk a lot about money dates. Because money," she said, pausing to let it land, "is on the same frequency as love, joy, and happiness."

Around the circle, the energy shifted. Everyone leaned in, journals temporarily forgotten.

"Like I shared on Day One," she continued, "having a healthy relationship with money and yourself is the only way to truly have prosperity. Just like you would nurture a romantic relationship, taking time to listen, connect, and understand, we must do the same with our money. A money date is not just about paying bills. It's about tuning in, listening, and aligning with your financial purpose."

She looked around the room at us, making sure we understood the concept.

"Think of it like getting ready for a typical date," she continued, her lips curving into a knowing smile. "You don't rush in wearing yesterday's clothes with tangled hair. You pick an outfit that makes you feel amazing, light a candle, maybe pour a glass of wine to chill before going. You take the time to look and feel your best. Your money deserves that same attention. That same respect."

She let the words linger, glancing around the circle as the women inched closer. "When you approach money this way, you're no longer avoiding it. You're inviting it in."

Then she lifted a stack of cream-colored cards with gold edging for everyone to see. "Here's what I want you to keep with you as a reminder of what's possible when you make time to date your money."

She read aloud from the top card:

Money Date – Block it in Your Calendar

- Clear your space
- Gratitude for every dollar that comes in
- Gratitude for every dollar that goes out (paying bills/committed expense)
- Visualize upcoming expenses + goals—tie them back to your financial purpose
- Call in aligned money and income
- Organize receipts, wallet, and invoices
- Celebrate your wins

"This is not about spreadsheets or shame. It's about energy. It's about setting the tone, choosing intention over chaos. It's about ownership and awareness," she said as she dropped a card on each of our tables. "It's about deciding to be powerful with your money."

Something clicked. "Thank you for this," I said, holding up my card. "I want to add that to my Prosperity Habit Stack. Wake up at seven, meditate for twenty minutes, get ready... and then, a one-hour money date. I think that sounds like a good start."

I could almost picture it: my first money date. A candle lit, soft music in the background, receipts stacked neatly instead of shoved in my purse. A cup of my favorite coffee in hand, as I opened my bank app, not with dread, but with curiosity. Gratitude. Power. For once, facing my money felt... almost intimate.

Lilly's smile softened, but there was something fierce behind it too—like she already saw the woman I could become.

"Roxanne, waking up early is your first domino. Everything else will flow from that. One shift creates momentum. And when you are in sync with your money and your financial purpose... magic happens. You'll start attracting everything you desire, with ease."

Stacking these habits wasn't just about routines—it was about stacking pieces of the woman I was finally ready to become.

I felt something loosen inside me. Like I could finally exhale. For the first time since landing in Bali, this whole money transformation thing felt... doable.

I didn't feel like I needed to fix my life. I felt like I was finally stepping into the woman I'd always known was waiting for me.

***

Discover how to create your domino habit.
You will find this mini exercise on page 211.

Chapter 12

Rising Up

Zoe

I woke up before the sun, the promise of a new day lingering in the air.

That alone felt like a miracle.

I had never been a morning person—at least not in the way people described it. I didn't leap out of bed with a bright smile and a clear goal or welcome the morning with positive affirmations. Mornings used to be a bleak reminder of my empty life, where I'd stretch myself thin for people too self-absorbed to notice. Then, completely exhausted, I would end the day knowing tomorrow would be the same.

But this morning was different. For once, there was no frantic rush, and no one needed my attention. There were no children to make lunches for and shuttle to and from school, no work emails pinging constantly, no pretending to be fine when I was clearly falling apart. Just this moment. Just me.

After pulling on my white tank top and black yoga pants, I made my way to the villa's patio, my journal pressed against my side. The early morning air, heavy with dew, brushed against my skin as the sky stretched above, washed in the best way—smoky purple and streaked with vibrant gold. I exhaled, feeling the tension leave my body. The world hadn't fully woken up yet. And for once, neither had the part of me that worried about everything.

With each step on the beach path, the cool sand squished beneath my feet, and the salty air invigorated me. I settled into a lounge chair near the edge of the beach, where I could watch the water gently kiss the shore. I tucked my knees under my chin and just watched, still and silent.

This was my first day of changing my habits. Lilly's words from yesterday's session echoed through me like a mantra: *Change your patterns, change your life.* It felt simple, but powerful. I had made a promise to myself—wake up early, journal, practice gratitude, and move my body.

I closed my eyes and let the hum of the ocean anchor me.

Stillness. Peace. Joy.

Then the vibration came.

I looked down at my phone lighting up beside me.

"You're so selfish. Even the kids can see that. They say you've changed. But that's a lie. Congrats. You're winning at being a shitty mom."

A knot formed in my stomach with a speed that robbed me of my breath. I used to think I would grow immune to Mark's words, which had become increasingly bitter since I kicked him out of the house. After all, how many times can someone try to hurt you with their sharp comments before you grow numb to them? But somehow, no matter what I did, these messages still sliced through my heart with a painful sting.

I could hear his voice even though it was just text. The anger, the blame, the twisted narrative where I was the villain for choosing myself.

The phone felt heavy in my hand as I picked it up, my thumb hovering over it. The unopened message felt heavy, a weight I didn't want, so I placed the phone face down beside me. I looked up at the ocean. The first rays of sunlight danced on the water's surface, and I inhaled deeply, letting the salty, clean air fill my lungs.

Lilly's story came flooding back—the way she told us about her first husband, who had diminished her, disrespected her, and drained her spirit. How she had run herself ragged fixing his messes, cushioning his ego, parenting him while trying to raise a family. Then, he abandoned her and her children with not enough resources to survive.

Her rock bottom.

She hadn't just hit it. She'd built her foundation on it.

"The only way to transform my reality was to change myself, not others or the environment around me," she had told us. Her voice was calm but fierce. "That's when I learned about queen energy and started acting like one. Not because I felt like one—but because I was tired of playing the victim."

I remembered that line; its meaning was crystal clear now. It settled into my soul, filling me with a profound sense of empowerment. Having hit rock bottom myself, I, too, am reclaiming my power, using it as a solid foundation to build a vibrant, new life.

I looked down at the new ring on my finger. The larimar glinted softly in the morning light, the gold band warm against my skin. The etched sunburst caught the sunrise and threw it back at me.

That ring was a stake in the ground. A declaration that I was worth it.

But in this moment—reading my ex's words, letting the hurt rise and fall like a tide—I realized I hadn't yet extended that worthiness to every part of my life.

Especially not to him.

The ring made me feel different and reminded me I had grown and changed. But he still triggered and tested me.

New level, new devil.

I remember hearing Lilly say that one night at dinner. Every stage of inner evolution introduces another test, showing where you're still vulnerable and need to grow. They are a gift, yet they sting like a punishment.

This may be a new devil, but I have reached a new level.

This text won't pull me down into its dark spiral. Defending myself would be futile to a man who was out of control and didn't see the truth of the situation. I will not replay old fights in my mind or waste time drafting a clever response I'll never send.

Instead, I looked out over the ocean, the sun peaking over the horizon, placed one hand on my heart, and whispered, "I'm not who I used to be." The wind caught my words and carried them.

I turned to my journal and started to write. My pen moved slowly, each word spilling out in my messy morning handwriting.

Today I am grateful for:

1. *Being by the ocean's quiet power—my soul is so happy.*

2. *The warmth of my new ring as it symbolizes a new beginning.*
3. *Waking up early to watch the beautiful sunrise.*
4. *Not answering the text message. I am so proud of myself!!!!!*
5. *My courage to sit with the discomfort instead of running from it.*

I re-read my words, closed my eyes, and drew in a slow, deliberate breath, letting the gratitude I'd just written sink deeper, as if every cell in my body could taste it.

I felt a soothing calm soften something deep inside me. That tight, clenched version of myself, who used to bend over backward to keep the peace, was slowly unfolding, ready to stand tall. Maybe I was finally ready to lead my own life for myself.

I wasn't so naïve to think this feeling of alignment, so sharp and clear in

this moment, wouldn't be tested down the line. There will be days when the urge to numb, to scroll endlessly on Instagram, or to wallow in my bottle of pinot grigio will creep back. But for now, I had momentum, and it was all that mattered.

And then I remembered what Lilly said. "It is easy to be grateful for the golden moments—the coffee, the laughter, the sunsets. But the real power comes when you can thank the hard things, too. The mess, the heartbreak, the moments that feel impossible. That's where life begins to shift."

I could almost hear the ocean and Lilly's voice blending together.

"Thank the mess. Thank the magic. Thank it all," she'd said, her tone soft yet certain. "Gratitude is how you rise—unshakable and unstoppable."

My ex wasn't the villain. The text wasn't the trap.

The real threat was betraying myself again. And I wasn't going to let that happen. This was the beginning. Of me. Of more. Of worthiness.

One sunrise at a time.

My chest swelled, feeling lighter than it had in years, as if the ocean itself had lifted a weight I didn't know I had been carrying. A tear slipped free, warm against the morning breeze—not from sadness, but from the quiet, undeniable truth that I could rise, too.

I curled my fingers around the ring, pressed it to my heart, and whispered, "I am worthy of it all."

And the water, as if it already knew, shimmered in agreement.

***

Make gratitude a daily ritual. Learn more on page 213.

Chapter 13

Mindful Money Solution

Julie

I woke up with my eyes swollen, puffy enough that blinking felt like an effort. The ceiling fan hummed overhead, moving the warm air in slow circles. The Bali sun was already bleeding through the gauzy curtains, far too bright for how heavy I felt inside.

At this retreat, I sat for three days in silence, pretending to scribble notes so I wouldn't have to utter a single word. Three days of making myself small, invisible, hiding in plain sight. My plan was to slip through the retreat unnoticed.

And yet... I'd listened to women speaking truths that left the air charged and heavy with unspoken emotion, then light again with relief. Their vulnerability had planted a seed: *maybe it was safe to be seen here.* Their unwavering courage inspired me to rethink my original plan of fading into the background.

Despite everything, a small part of me wished I could just go back home. I needed the security of a mindless routine, a place where I could disappear from my heartbreaking story and the sad, knowing looks people gave me. My mind turned to my boys, Lucas and Noah. Were they eating breakfast? Had they fought? Did they miss me, or were they quietly angry that I had left?

But even as the thought crossed my mind, I knew I couldn't go home. My friend, Pattie, had begged me to take this trip. She'd promised to watch the boys, and she'd been so certain that I needed this space—for me, for them, for the future none of us could yet see.

I sat on the edge of the bed, feeling the cool and smooth tiles beneath my bare feet. My suitcase lay open on the chair, still half-unpacked, clothes in muted colors I had worn for years. It had been ages since I had purchased something new—there was neither the time nor a compelling reason to do so.

Walking to the suitcase, I caught my reflection in the mirror. Long, limp brown hair framed my pale face, with roots laced with silver that I had given up hiding. Eyes that used to sparkle were now dull and ringed with shadows. I no longer recognized the face I saw in the mirror. I had been so focused on holding my boys together after their father's death that I didn't realize how much I was falling apart. Grief etched lines onto my face and weighed heavily on my spirit, making me look and feel sixty instead of forty-five.

I pulled out a loose, sleeveless navy dress, the kind that hides a soft middle, and slipped it over my head. I struggled to quiet the part of me that wanted to hide in this room all day instead of going to the retreat. My sandals sat by the door, a silent invitation to go. And I needed to, for my own well-being and for the sake of my sons.

I anchored myself, took a deep breath, and said with a determined voice, "I am brave, I am strong, I can do this."

This was the mantra that had gotten me through the months of watching my husband disappear before my eyes and finally take his last breath. It was a lifeline, a steady hand pushing me on when I wanted to give up.

The walk to the retreat pavilion was warm and fragrant, with frangipani blossoms scattered like little offerings along the stone path.

The sky was already bright, the heat rising in waves and pressing gently against my skin. My sandals slapped softly as I walked, each step a small return to myself.

Up ahead, I passed a father laughing as he spun his son in circles. The boy squealed with joy, his tiny hands gripping his dad's wrists like it was the safest place in the world.

Something in my chest caught, not a full ache, but a flicker of something sharp and familiar. I looked away, quickly, and kept walking. That used to be us. Ryan took turns tossing the boys into the air while I watched from the porch, heart full and whole. Now I am here. Alone.

I felt the sting of tears rise, uninvited. But instead of pushing it down, I whispered the words Lilly had shared on Day One: "This is your moment to learn, grow, and expand."

I didn't need to collapse into sadness. I just needed to notice it. To hold it. To keep walking.

Inside, a cool breeze swept through the hall from the ocean, a welcome respite from the heat. I settled into my usual spot at the circle's edge, trying to fade into the background. I loved the delicate fragrance of fresh lotus flowers sitting in a vase on my table, mingling with the subtle, earthy scent of the incense burning at the front of the room. Taking a deep, calming breath, I settled in while pretending to be engrossed in my journal to avoid any conversation.

Lilly was already standing at the front of the room, barefoot in a flowing soft pink tunic, her presence filling the space. I had watched her for three days now, noticing her subtle way of holding a room without overpowering it. It fascinated me how the women seemed to lean into her words like flowers turning to the sun.

"Today," she announced with a smile, "we are changing it up a bit. I thought it would be amazing to save our yoga session for tonight, on the beach as the sun sets."

A few women nodded, while others shared enthusiastic yeses, their faces lit up with excitement. I sat quietly, indifferent, as the thought of yoga at any time filled me with a quiet dread. I didn't get the appeal of twisting and bending into a pretzel, feeling the strain in every muscle.

Lilly smiled at us, a wide, genuine smile, and said, "I am pleased you all seem to enjoy that idea. Let's get this session started, then. I would like to start with a quick recap. Over the past few days, we have explored how money is a tool, how shifting your mindset can begin to untangle old beliefs, and how building a wealthy self-image invites you to take up space in your own life. From there, we have begun creating a vision rooted in purpose and stacking small habits that support who you are becoming. Each step builds the foundation for what comes next."

She let the words settle, then added, "Now, I would like you to reflect on this: What's one recent money situation that felt overwhelmingly stressful for you, and how did you handle it?"

The air shifted. Some women glanced at each other; others stared at the floor. My shoulders tensed. Overwhelming? Try suffocating. Since Ryan died, my entire relationship with money has been a disorienting fog I cannot navigate, leaving me lost and unsure of my future. He had handled it all, the monthly bills, our investments, and all the tough financial decisions. He tried to teach me a couple of times, but a mental block would always form, and I would put it off for another day. I convinced myself I wasn't good with numbers, after all, I was in the people business as a Human Resource manager, and that money was *his* thing. Looking back, it was always my dad's job, and my mom encouraged me to find a man with a great job and pension so he could take care of me.

Now Ryan is gone. And in his absence, money from the life insurance policy arrived in my life like a guest I didn't invite and didn't know how to host. Afraid of mishandling it and losing everything, I just left the life insurance check in my dresser drawer. A tear slid down my cheek, and I tried to control my breathing. I gripped my pen, hoping Lilly wouldn't notice.

"Julie," Lilly said gently, "are you okay?"

My chest squeezed. Part of me wanted to nod, but I shook my head instead. My voice came out thinner than I expected.

"I… I've been avoiding all of it," I said. "My husband passed away a year ago, and when he did, there was… money. More than I ever imagined I would have. But I don't know what to do with it. I feel stupid that I never learned. And scared I will get it wrong. He tried to teach me but…" I swallowed hard. "…But I put it off and then there wasn't time."

The room was quiet. No pity, just stillness.

Lilly nodded. "Thank you for trusting us with that, Julie. I know that was hard for you to share out loud. This is exactly why we are here. And you are not alone. I'm going to walk us through something today—a way to feel calm, clear, and confident with your money. It's not a budget… It's a system built on purpose. And Julie… If you're okay with it, we'll use your story to bring it to life."

I swallowed. "Okay."

She moved to the whiteboard and wrote in bold letters: *The Mindful Money Solution*. The marker squeaked as she underlined it twice.

"*The Mindful Money Solution* is a six-step system I created that will help you gain confidence in your financial decisions, control your cash flow, give you clarity around your financial purpose, and make spending stress-free. I perfected it during my twenty years as a wealth advisor. This is so powerful, I can't wait to go through the steps with all of you. Remember, your money will flow where you want it to go."

Lilly walked towards me.

"The first step is to determine your financial purpose, which we discussed on Day One. So, Julie... Would you like to share with the group what *your* financial purpose is?"

My mind scrambled for the right answer. The truth is, I never finished the homework Lilly gave us. I had been too foggy that day, too overwhelmed to think clearly. I blurted out the first thing that came to mind. "Security for my boys." Then, softer, almost a whisper, "And... Freedom for *me*."

I paused. My stomach twisted.

"Before I met Ryan," I said slowly, "I had accumulated a lot of debt. He was amazing and had it paid down so quickly. He helped us buy our home, and he built a life with me."

I had never shared the part of my story about debt with anyone else. Only Ryan knew the weight of that shame, and not once did he ever make me feel like less of a person for carrying it.

My throat tightened.

"Now that he's gone, I'm the one who has to hold it all together. And honestly, I'm terrified. I'm so afraid I'll fall back into those old patterns. That I'll end up drowning in debt again. I don't want to live in fear anymore. I don't want to go back to that version of me."

Lilly smiled. "I know that wasn't easy for you to share, Julie. Remember this is a safe space and we are here to support you on your journey."

Security for your boys, that is your compass, she wrote this on the board.

"Without a purpose, money decisions are often made from impulse-driven decisions rooted in fear, guilt, or shame. Your purpose becomes your filter. Every choice runs through the question: *Does this move me toward my purpose, or away from it?*"

This isn't just about keeping the lights on, then, I thought. It's about building the life I actually want, the life my kids and I deserve.

"The next step in the *Mindful Money Solution* is knowing your monthly income. Do you know what yours is, Julie?" Lilly asked.

"Not really... I've been avoiding looking at anything," I admitted.

"Avoidance is a shield against overwhelm and insecurity," she said, trying to sound reassuring. "But confidence in your money situation comes from awareness. Imagine driving without knowing how much gas is in the tank, the anxiety building with every mile. How would it feel to be in that situation?" she asked me.

"That would be so stressful," I answered.

"A stress...like the nagging worry of not understanding where your money goes?" she asked, her smirk playful and knowing. "When you know your numbers, you lead from a place of solid confidence, feeling empowered instead of acting out of fear, doubt, or worry."

I felt my shoulders drop a little. *I could do that. One number. That's it.*

"Did you feel that shift in your energy, Julie? Knowing you are starting to have a plan to tackle your finances, the stress melts away."

I nodded in agreement. I felt lighter, as if a weight had been lifted from my shoulders. And maybe even more confident. I wasn't sure; it had been so long since I had last felt truly confident.

"Okay," Lilly said, her eyes scanning the circle. "I want to ask something, and I want you to be really honest—not with me, but with yourself. Please raise your hand if you can tell me your exact monthly income right now."

It surprised me when only Barb, with a confident grin, put up her hand. I looked around the room. I was shocked that the other women weren't fully aware of the details of their finances. I thought I was the only one.

"Knowing your income is key, so you can clearly see what funds are available to fuel your purpose and ensure you are comfortably covering all your expenses while enjoying your daily lives. With a set salary, the number is easy to figure out with just a quick glance at your bank account. Self-employed individuals may need extra time to calculate this, so if you don't know for sure, put down your best estimate for now. You can work on calculating the exact total amount when you get back home," Lilly explained.

"Now that I think about it, I do know I receive about $3,600 in my bank account approximately every two weeks. Does that work?"

She walked back to the whiteboard and wrote the numbers in green. "Yes, that is perfect, Julie."

"Once you know your financial purpose and your income, the third step is to organize and separate your money into different purpose accounts. The number of accounts will vary depending on your own purposes, not anyone else's," she stated with certainty.

"Julie, you said that your purpose is to provide security for Lucas and Noah. Can you break this down further into what that means for you?"

"Hmmm, I hadn't thought of it, to be honest." I paused, closed my eyes, and took a deep breath to feel in my heart what I really want to have happen. "Security would mean my mortgage is paid off, that the boys and I can go on a nice vacation every year, I'm able to pay for their education, and I think the last would be to have enough saved in case of an emergency."

As I spoke each purpose out loud, Lilly was completing the flow chart for me in front of all the women, making me feel naked and vulnerable as each word was showing up.

She turned back to me.

"To be honest, Lilly... the insurance money is still sitting in my savings account. It's supposed to pay off the mortgage. But I haven't had the courage to go to the bank."

The silence held me, but didn't rush me.

"I know it's ridiculous," I added quickly, "But every time I even think about touching that money... it's like... it makes it final. Like he's really, really gone. And I'm not ready for that. I think I've been afraid that if I use it, I'll mess it up. That I won't know what I'm doing. That I'll screw up this gift he left us."

Lilly didn't speak right away. She moved in close, crouched beside me, and rested her hand gently on mine, grounding me. Her voice was soft, but steady.

"Julie... that money isn't a goodbye," she said, "it's a bridge. A bridge between what was and what's next. It's the gift he left to carry you forward. To help you and the boys *live*—not just survive. When you're ready, using that money won't mean letting go of him. It'll be choosing to stand for yourself. For your future. For the life he trusted you to build."

She paused, letting the words land. Gently wiping away my tears, I could feel the tightness in my chest loosen.

"You're doing amazing, Julie. Are you ready to move on?"

I drew in a slow, steady breath, the kind that filled me all the way through. Then, without needing to speak, I let my chin dip—small, but certain. A quiet yes. Not just to the next step. To myself.

"By opening separate accounts representing each of your purposes, you can easily organize your finances and reach your goals. Most financial institutions allow you to set up multiple accounts and label them so you can keep track of and see each purpose grow, becoming more of a reality. This is like paying yourself first, the most fundamental principle in personal finance. It means you treat each purpose as a priority and fund these accounts before you spend money on anything."

Lilly looked at me. "Julie, when you get back home, you will open three purpose savings accounts, one for vacation, one for emergencies—or what I call a *prosperity cushion*—and the last for the boy's education; perhaps this one would be more of an investment rather than a savings account. You'll allocate a certain amount of dollars per account when you get paid. How does that sound?"

I laughed. "Easier than what I thought."

Several of the other women laughed and nodded in agreement.

"The fourth step in this strategy is to break down your expenses into two types, one for your fixed, recurring expenses—for example, your mortgage or rent, insurance, utilities, debt, etc. Just go through your bills, list them and calculate the total. The total dollar amount goes to this fixed expenses account with each paycheck."

At home, I pictured the stack of papers on my husband's desk. I didn't know the total off hand, but I knew I could do the simple math it would take to figure it out.

"The second type of expenses is for your personal spending, which is where the rest of your money goes. This will be the account for your groceries, entertainment, personal grooming, clothes, and anything else you choose to spend your money on."

I chuckled as I looked down at my well-worn dress. "It's been a while since I've spent any money on clothing."

"Wish I was more like you," Roxanne said, her smile bright and genuine.

That triggered another round of laughter. I felt myself loosening up, as if the weight of figuring this out by myself lifted, and sharing my story felt less agonizing.

"With the personal spending account, you can use a variety of ways to access your money—your debit card, cash, or a reloadable card where you can only spend the money you've already loaded onto it," Lilly added.

She went to the whiteboard and started writing. "With Julie's examples, there are now five accounts—three savings accounts for her purposes of education, vacation, and prosperity cushion, and two checking accounts for her fixed and personal expenses."

She listed them one by one.

"Picture your money, Julie, as guests cheerfully arriving at a spacious house with five cozy rooms. The guests know exactly where they belong. No one wanders the hallway, wondering where to go. That's how you keep everything in its place and ensure peace of mind."

A surprising wave of relief passed through me. *That... I could visualize. That made sense.*

"As you calculate your numbers," Lilly said, her eyes sparkling, "you'll begin to align your spending with what truly matters to you—what brings you joy and reflects your values. It is all about priorities. For instance, I love the experience of buying new clothes way more than the momentary satisfaction of eating out, so more of my spending account goes there. But my friend is a dedicated foodie; she would wear a burlap sack if it meant getting the best table at her favorite restaurant." Lilly's smile softened. "The point is: spend consciously. Let your money reflect what lights you up—not what numbs you for a moment and leaves regret behind."

She walked to the whiteboard, wrote the word "taxes," and circled it several times. "This is important. You do not want to get behind on your taxes. If you are employed, they are deducted automatically. For those of you who own a business, it is your responsibility to pay the government, whether you want to or not."

We all laughed.

"I know," Lilly said. "No one enjoys paying taxes, but when we do, what it means is that we have made money."

I nodded in agreement and noticed the others did, too.

Lilly stepped away from the board and walked into the center of the room.

"I know this is a lot to process, but once you have completed each of these four steps, you can then automate everything, which is the next step in the *Mindful Money Solution*. This is the part where most people breathe easier," she said. "Decide the amounts to flow to each account. Then, set up automatic transfers from your income account into each category every month. You'll never have to stress over what to do in any situation or be overwhelmed by your personal finances."

"So I wouldn't have to keep asking myself, *Should I?* or *Can I?* The system would already know?" I asked. "That would make things so much easier."

"I totally agree," said Mikayla.

"That's the whole point," Lilly said. "It is about making prosperity easy."

She smiled and turned back to the board.

"Step six is one of the most important and one of my personal favorites: setting up a money date. Roxanne brought this up yesterday. As a review, pick a consistent time that works for you and sets you up for success. For me, I do this every Friday and block off an hour in my day before I start working. You could even include your boys if you want, Julie. That would set them up with a great financial education. Also, remember to have it in a welcoming space—make it pleasant, like you would do for an actual date. I like to light a candle, pour myself some tea, and play my favorite music. You're not simply budgeting—you're leading your life like a prosperous CEO leads a successful company."

I pictured it—just me, wearing a blue dress that would bring out my eyes, a steaming cappuccino next to me, and sunlight gleaming in the windows. When I get comfortable with the steps and it becomes more natural, I can invite Lucas and Noah to join in. For once, money was not a monster to hide from, but a conversation I could actually have.

By the time Lilly capped her marker, I realized my jaw had unclenched. My pen was resting loosely in my hand. My breathing had evened out.

Grief was still there—always there—but it no longer felt like it was the only thing in the room with me. Something else had arrived: a glimmer of clarity, a thread of possibility.

When the session ended, I stepped outside into sunlight that, despite the growing heat, felt softer than it had an hour ago. The frangipani's perfume wrapped around me, and the ocean's rhythm was steady in the distance.

For the first time since arriving, I didn't want to hide in my room.

For the first time since he died, I thought, *maybe I can do this.*

***

Now it's time to take that purpose and bring it to life. Head to page 215 to create a real, tangible system that supports you with clarity, ease, and joy.

Chapter 14

Building A Wealth Blueprint

Dorothy

Settling cross-legged on the cushion, journal at my side, my eyes were closed, but my mind was still racing.

The fourth day of the retreat had begun with guided meditation. Katie's soft voice faded into the background—murmuring about finding yourself, about your breath guiding you home—but my mind, restless and buzzing, refused to settle.

My hips ached with a dull, persistent throb. A strange tingling sensation ran through my feet. I was mentally juggling thoughts of what was going on at home with deciding which pictures of Bali I wanted to post on Facebook to impress my friends. Then, a question popped into my mind: *How did I even get here?*

My mind wandered back to a memory of standing at the window in my kitchen the week before I left for Bali with my hands wrapped around a warm mug of coffee. I watched the sun creep over the quiet street. The house felt... still. My daughter, Keeler, proudly owned her own condo, while my son, Aidan, had moved out last spring, embarking on his own adventure with friends in Costa Rica. The hum of the fridge was the loudest thing in the room.

My husband, Jason, was off on another boys' weekend. Golf this time. What started as a rare treat slowly morphed into regular, almost monthly trips over the years. He left. I stayed home. We weren't fighting. It simply became the rhythm of our current life.

I managed the house, paid the bills, bought the groceries, kept in touch with the kids, and maintained our extended family's calendar. We'd made the decision together because I was honestly better at it. But somehow, I had built a life where it was expected of me to manage everyone *else's* needs before I thought of my own.

I took another sip of coffee and thought about the morning walks I had started with my friends. We strolled through the quiet neighborhood in the early hours, the air crisp and still, the sky painted in soft pinks and oranges. We had conversations that surprised me. They weren't about the latest sales at the local shops, or recipes, or the weather forecast. They were deep, meaningful conversations. My friends shared health scares, marriages quietly unravelling, and secret dreams whispered for the first time, full of hope and vulnerability.

At sixty-two and as a confident sales executive, you would think I'd be comfortable sharing my deepest secrets with these women. But most mornings, I would push my hands deeper into my cozy Patagonia puffer jacket I snagged on Facebook Marketplace, tuck my silver bob under my warm hat, and just listen to the conversations around me. That was my role. The friend who absorbed the pain of others but never added her own.

And yet, somewhere along those early morning walks, something shifted. Not loudly. Not suddenly. But two questions nagged at me: *If I allowed myself to speak freely, what would I share? Who would I be if I lived for me?*

There were so many moments in the conversation when I could have spoken about losing my mom and about how she died when I was forty, right at the time I needed her most. I was raising two toddlers, already stretched thin and overwhelmed by life. Then she got sick, and everything became a blur of hospital visits, Jason's endless traveling, and children's coughs and runny noses. I tried to be with her as much as I could, but it was never enough. She slipped away so quickly.

One of the last things we talked about was regret. She carried so many of them. My mother begged me to live my life fully, not to put things off, not to wait. She said if I did, I'd end up like her—looking back at everything I'd missed. To help my father build his business, he had put her dreams on hold. And when it failed, she was the one left to pick up the pieces while he walked away.

She was only a year older than I am now when she died. It was time I did something about the long list of things I wanted to do in my life.

That evening, it was Keeler who nudged me over the edge. "Mom," she'd said, curling her legs under her on my couch, "when are you going to do something for yourself?"

I shrugged. "What would I even do?"

She looked at me, eyes soft. "I don't know. But maybe stop waiting for permission to do something."

Later that night, while scrolling through Instagram, I paused on a video from a woman named Lilly Ainsworth talking about her women's retreat in Bali.

"Permission," she said. "No one will hand it to you. You have to give it to yourself."

The words resonated deeply in my soul.

In that moment, eager for change, I booked the retreat. Bali. A full week. Just me. After 30 years of obligations, I finally prioritized my own desires and did something for myself.

The sharp squawk of a bird from the balcony jolted me back from my memories to the pavilion. I opened my eyes. The other women seemed deep in meditation, with eyes closed and their bodies perfectly still. I shut my eyes again. I wasn't meditating. But something had landed, that final piece clicking into place, and I was finally ready to listen—to Lilly, yes. But also, for the first time, to myself.

***

Later that morning, after we put away the meditation cushions and returned to our seats, Lilly stood at the front of the room, her presence calm and grounded, as if she had built a whole life on the other side of saying yes to herself.

She picked up a marker and wrote across the whiteboard in bold, steady strokes: *The Wealth Blueprint.*

"Your wealth," she said, "isn't just what's in your accounts. It is how you live. It is how your money either supports your values or slowly erodes them. Does everyone remember our conversation about *Mindful Money Solution* yesterday?" she asked. Heads nodded. Pens lifted. "That's the foundation of your *Wealth Blueprint.* Remember, if you haven't figured out what your income is yet, that's your homework for when you go home. Without cash flow clarity, everything else stands on shaky ground."

She smiled gently, then drew a 3D house on the board, a simple sketch with four solid walls and space for a roof. Underneath it, she wrote, *Mindful Money Solution.*

"Imagine trying to build a house without a blueprint. Walls might go up, but nothing would align. One powerful storm, and it would crumble. Your life works the same way. Without a blueprint, life just... happens to you. But with one, you become the architect. You design something that will last, something that reflects you."

I leaned in and noticed the other women did as well.

"Today, we are going to discuss the four walls that hold your financial life upright." She tapped each of the four walls with her marker.

"Tomorrow we will cover insurance and protection—that's the roof."

She paused for a moment.

"Before we discuss what each of these walls represents," Lilly said," I want you to imagine five, ten, or even twenty years from now. What does your life look like? Where are you? What are you doing with your time? And most importantly, how does the way you manage your money support that vision?"

The question hit me with surprising force. I looked down at my lap, and a wave of anxiety made my throat tighten. Tears suddenly sprang to my eyes, blurring my vision. Then, before I knew it, I raised my hand.

Lilly nodded at me as she walked toward me.

"How can you imagine your life in five years when you've spent your whole life making sure everyone else is okay? I juggled small kids, climbed the corporate ladder, and still did all the caregiving. I organized holidays, ran the household, remembered birthdays, paid the bills, cooked the meals..."

My voice trailed off, overwhelmed by vulnerability.

I took a calming breath and continued. "My husband goes golfing during the weekdays or goes away on weekends with his friends. This is on top of work trips. He always has. I stayed behind for the kids and to keep the house running because I thought that is what good mothers do... what good wives do." My eyes blurred with tears. "But lately I've been wondering, is that selfless? Or am I just afraid to ask for more? Maybe I played small because that felt safer than admitting I needed something more."

Lilly put a hand on my shoulder. "That realization," she said softly, "is the beginning of your blueprint."

A shaky laugh escaped. "I didn't even know I could have a blueprint."

"You can," Lilly replied. "We all can and should. And it's time."

She walked back to the flip chart. On one wall, she wrote *Retirement*. "Your retirement plan funds your future self's life."

She turned to me. "Dorothy, what does retirement look like for you?"

I hesitated. "Umm...maybe quiet mornings walking to my local coffee shop. A chance to read a book. Maybe travel?"

She smiled. "If that is what you want, are your current financial plans building *that* life, or just delaying it?"

I reflected on the years of contributions to the company pension and group retirement plan, never questioning the choice of investments, their performance, or their alignment with my goals. I had no idea what retirement investments Jason had made.

"To be honest, I'm not sure," I answered.

"When I was a wealth advisor, I noticed most people don't," Lilly said. "It is so important to be clear about what you want that chapter of your life to look like and then create a plan to get there. What you want may not be what someone like Sofia or Julie wants." She looked at each of them and smiled, then turned back to me. "Therefore, there is no one plan that fits all."

She looked up at the group. "In your journals, please write these two questions: What is the vision for my retirement? Does my current plan support this? Take your time with this. Your future self will thank you for it."

I wrote in my journal:

Define my retirement vision.
Check if my current plan supports it.

I added:

Have a conversation with Jason about his vision and plan.

Then, Lilly wrote *Tax Planning* on another wall of her diagram.

"This wall," she said, pointing to it with the marker, "is how you keep as much as you can of what you've earned."

I shifted slightly in my chair. My pay stub had always felt like a confusing mess of jargon—deductions, withholdings, pension amounts. The thought of questioning any of it never even crossed my mind. We sent all the tax information to our accountant with my silent prayer that I wouldn't have to pay more than what was already deducted.

"Tax planning isn't just for business owners," she continued. "It is important for everyone. The question you need to ask is, *How do I legally keep more of what I've worked so hard to earn, maximizing my financial freedom?* I would advise you to talk to an accountant or tax expert if you're not knowledgeable in those areas. It is amazing how a good tax strategy can bring more money into your pocket. It feels like finding free money without having to work any harder."

I wrote in my journal:

Talk to our accountant.
Create a tax strategy so we have more money without working harder.

Lilly drew a small heart over the front wall and then wrote *Estate Planning* underneath it.

"Estate planning isn't about death," she said. "It's about love. It's about ensuring your loved ones are cared for the way *you* want."

My chest tightened. We had not updated our wills since Keeler and Aidan were small, a time when our primary concern was the what-if scenario of needing someone to raise them. We had named my sister and her husband as guardians, who now live across the country and have kids of their own.

Lilly continued, "Any time life takes an unexpected turn, your official last will and testament should evolve to reflect those changes. Marriage, divorce, kids becoming adults, retirement, losing your spouse—every major shift in your life is a signal that your wishes may need to be updated. Your will is your voice for when you're no longer here. And if it doesn't reflect the life you're living now, it may not serve the people you love the way you hope it would. And if you don't have a will? Your voice won't be heard at all."

"I know this isn't easy to talk about for anyone," Lilly said softly. "I am sure this is extra hard for you, Julie." Lilly looked over at her, placed her hand on her heart, and took a moment before continuing. "But if you have a will that clearly reflects your wishes, it allows your family to grieve in peace, instead of being burdened by figuring out what to do with your estate—or worse, fighting over it."

Lilly continued. "And just as important is having a power of attorney, someone you trust to make financial or health decisions on your behalf if you are unable to. Think of it as choosing a trusted hand to hold the wheel if, for some reason, you cannot steer your own ship. Life can change in an instant—illness, an accident, or simply age catching up. If you choose a good power of attorney, he or she will make the right financial or health decisions to honor your wishes. This is especially vital if you are single, and even more so if you have minor children. Without it, strangers or the courts may end up deciding who takes the helm without regard to what you wanted."

A palpable shift in energy silenced the room. The air was thick with a heavy, somber silence. I wrote:

Talk to the kids.
Review our beneficiaries.
Meet with a lawyer.
Update our wills and powers of attorney.

On the last wall, she wrote Investments. "This is the last and most important step. This is where your money grows," Lilly said, tapping at the drawn wall with the marker. "Therefore, it is important to ensure you have the right investments that match with your financial purpose. This is where we personalize your strategy. Your investment plan should be as unique as you are."

She wrote beside the house:

Financial Purpose + Time Frame + Risk Tolerance = Investment Strategy

"These three ingredients," she said, "are how we decide what to invest in. And therefore, I always recommend working with a trusted professional advisor. There are so many options—so many vehicles—and your needs deserve careful consideration."

She listed a few examples on the board:

- Registered vs. Non-Registered Accounts
- Short-term vs. Long-term Vehicles
- High-risk vs. Low-risk Investments

"If retirement is still fifteen or twenty years away, you have time on your side. That means you can take a little more risk, like owning stocks, exchange-traded funds, or even mutual funds. Yes, they'll rise and fall along the way, but over the years, those ups and downs begin to even out.

Historically, they've grown more than safer investments, which can make a big difference in how much your nest egg grows by the time you're ready for your next chapter. It's like standing at the edge of the ocean: The waves may rush forward and pull back, sometimes further than you'd like, but the tide always returns. And over time, it carries more to the shore than it takes away."

She paused.

"But if you need your money in a year or two—say, for a down payment or a big trip—you might choose lower-risk or even no-risk investments. The returns may be smaller, but they protect your capital from any volatility."

Then she added something that made it all click for me.

"Because you have different financial goals—each with different time frames—you'll likely have different investment accounts to match. Your retirement fund would be separate from your short-term savings for that dream vacation or a future wedding. Give each goal a place to grow that is best suited for it."

I nodded at Lilly's words. "I thought about how many times I had said, 'Whatever you think is best,' when my husband wanted to talk to me about our investments. I didn't understand it all, and it seemed too overwhelming to learn. But now I see it differently. I had opted out of my own financial story. I haven't thought about cash flow and taxes. And I know we need to change our wills. I've got a lot to learn," I said with a long sigh. "And I need to decide what I want to do with my life, so I don't have regrets, like my mom."

"Yes, Dorothy! A life with no regrets is a life well-lived. Let's aim for that, everybody," Lilly said, beaming.

My pen hovered for a moment. I thought of that conversation I'd had with Aidan, about how wonderful it would be to take the whole family on a trip to Ireland someday—to show them where my grandparents had lived, to walk those hills with my future grandchildren at my side.

I scribbled in the margins:

Ireland trip fund.

Just seeing it written made it feel more real.

I copied Lilly's next words:

You're not just investing your money. You're investing in your future—and it's worth doing with clarity, confidence, and support.

I jotted down:

Review our portfolios.

Make sure they align with our purpose.
Set up an Ireland fund.

Lilly capped her marker and looked around the circle. "Look at your four walls. Where are the cracks? Where is the structure strong?"

I looked down at my journal—at the house I'd sketched, simple but clear. Four walls, each now alive with meaning and purpose. I was excited to build this house.

***

Later that afternoon, after the session ended, I sat by the edge of the infinity pool. The sky was golden, and the sea hummed below, quiet and sure. My journal was open beside me, but I hadn't touched it yet.

My phone buzzed. Jason.

I hadn't expected a message, as the geographical distance had seemed to amplify our emotional disconnection.

I've been thinking about you all day. I'm proud of you for going. I know this retreat was a big step, but you did it, and I really admire that.

I miss you.

Tears stung my eyes. We hadn't fought. We'd just... drifted. This was so out of character that I didn't even know how to respond.

And then it hit me. He had been our financial warrior all of these years, and I never appreciated it. I took a deep breath and started typing.

I've been thinking about you, too. And I just want to say… thank you for all the ways you've carried our finances over the years. Because of you, we are mortgage-free. We put our kids through school. We can help with future weddings. You've done an incredible job, and I've never said it enough. Being here has shown me how rare that is. And how I've opted out of being part of it. I want to be your financial partner now. I want us to plan our next chapter—together. I want something that gives you your weekends with the guys, me with my girlfriends, and time for us to travel together. And maybe even one big trip a year with the kids.

I pushed the send button. A moment passed before he replied.

That sounds amazing. I miss you, Dorothy. I can't wait until you're home so we can get started on this.

I pressed a hand to my heart and closed my eyes.

Picture her, Lilly had said. *The woman you're becoming.*

And I saw *her*.

In five years, I imagine myself strolling hand-in-hand with Jason on Ireland's cobblestone streets, our grandchildren's laughter echoing in the air behind us.

I opened my journal and wrote:

Our life. Our wealth. Our way.

And then I put a big heart underneath and closed the book.

***

To reflect on how strong your wealth blueprint is, go to page 217.

Chapter 15

Are You Covered?

Zoe

Predawn has become one of my favorite times of the day, the moment before darkness gives way to light. The sky shifts like a kaleidoscope, each second unveiling a new pattern of pink, blue, violet, and orange. It feels alive, never the same, always moving.

I live on this planet with millions of people, yet at this moment, it feels like I am the only one awake, the only one bearing witness to the daily masterpiece of the rising sun.

I breathe in the salty air, and the gratitude fills me until it overflows. I am here, in Bali, feeling a calm I didn't know was even possible. A peace I have never known before has quieted the noise of my ex's insults and has given me the space to find my voice and embrace who I am, deep down.

Being here, surrounded by Lilly and the group, has shifted my mindset and how I view my mistakes. Listening to them each tell their stories with honesty and courage, without apology, has inspired me to do the same.

While basking in the beauty of the sunrise, I flipped through my journal and found my notes from the wealthy self-image session.

One line from Lilly jumped out at me:

Your attention is drawn to what's meant for you—what your soul desires.

I paused, letting that settle. Then I read on. Lilly had explained how judgment of others or ourselves can keep us locked in low-energy vibes, stuck in fear or insecurity. But instead of avoiding our judgments, she offered a new way to see them.

"Use them as mirrors," she had said. "If I judge someone for flaunting their wealth, maybe it's because I feel guilty about wanting more. If I roll my eyes at someone's confidence, maybe it's because I haven't fully owned mine."

Maybe making judgments about people has a positive aspect. They're clues, little windows into my own unhealed stories. And if I'm brave enough to look at them without shame, I can shift them. I can turn that energy into awareness and notice where I need to change my thoughts, feelings, and actions.

I closed my eyes, and a memory surfaced: The plane ride here. The moment I saw Lilly in her cream silk blouse with an emerald ring flashing on her finger, I judged her instantly. I thought she must have married into money and has no idea what struggle even looks like.

When I think of it now, it leaves a pit in my stomach. I cut her down in my mind when all she's doing is living her best life. She was heading here to Bali to guide us back to ourselves, holding up a mirror to our money stories and showing us how to rebuild with clarity and intention.

But the truth is, those judgments weren't about her. They were about me. My fear that I could never be that free, that radiant, that abundant. I was resentful that I was arriving in Bali broken in pieces, while she seemed so fulfilled and complete.

And I was judging her clothes, her confidence, her life because those are the very things I secretly want for myself, but had buried under resentment and fear.

And I knew exactly where some of that fear came from.

For years, my ex's words echoed in my ears: *You're just trying to keep up with the Joneses.* Or the time he criticized me for owning too many black shoes, when I only had two pairs. His judgment, disguised as jokes or warnings, held me back from the things I really wanted. I stopped trusting my own desires, second-guessing every purchase, every spark of joy, every dream that felt "too much."

And suddenly, sitting here with the sunrise stretching gold across the ocean, I saw the truth. Those judgments weren't mine. They were his. And I had carried them like stones in my backpack for years.

Did I want to feel radiant in my own skin? Yes.

Did I want to carry myself with the ease of a woman who knows who she is and what she wants? Absolutely.

Did I want a life that felt abundant, secure, beautiful? More than anything.

What I had dismissed as envy was really longing. And longing, I realized, is direction. It's my soul whispering, *This is possible for you, too.*

The thought gave me goose bumps. For the first time, instead of shrinking from my judgments—or his—I leaned into them. What if they weren't proof of my smallness, but a compass pointing toward what I truly want for my life?

The sun rose higher, making the waves sparkle like diamonds, and I let that possibility wash through me. I wrote in my journal to mark this moment.

A life of more: More freedom. More joy. More me.

The sun was high above the horizon when I headed towards the path that led to the pavilion. My journal was tucked under my arm, its pages filled with all the wisdom shared this week. I looked forward to the next sessions.

The whiteboard still showed Lilly's house sketch from yesterday afternoon. Four walls stood solid in marker: retirement, tax planning, estate planning, and investments. A few women were lingering by the beverage station, their laughter mixing with the hum of cicadas outside. I slipped into my seat, opening my journal to my last entry, ready to write more.

When everyone was seated, Lilly stood at the front of the room, hands clasped in front of her, eyes closed and taking a deep breath. Her presence always seemed to steady the room. She opened her eyes and smiled.

"Yesterday," she began, gesturing toward the diagram, "we built the walls of your Wealth Blueprint. Today, we will finish the house."

She turned and drew a triangular roof above the walls, writing one word inside: *Protection.*

"Our roof is our insurance," she said, gently. "It shields everything we have built from life's storms—illness, accidents... even death. Without it, your foundation and walls can be destroyed in a single moment."

She glanced around the circle, her tone softening. "Who here has felt their roof tested?"

The room stilled.

And then Lilly did something I didn't expect. She turned and walked over to Julie.

Her voice was quiet. "Before we go any further... I just want to take a moment for Julie. Because when we talk about protection, we are not just talking about numbers and policies. We are talking about love. Julie, you lived through what most of us fear, and your story is why this matters so deeply."

Julie blinked quickly, her lips pressed together. Lilly reached out and placed a hand over hers. "Thank you for being here. And thank you for showing us what real strength looks like." Only then did Lilly return her gaze to the group. "Can we all show Julie some love?"

The room erupted with applause. Dorothy stood up and walked over to hug her. Sofia leaned over and squeezed her arm.

Mikayla yelled out, "We love you, Julie!" Then she made the shape of a heart with her hands and smiled at her.

"We all do, Julie," Barb said, her voice thick with emotion. " And we're here for you now and for the rest of your life."

Julie wiped away a tear and then said, "I am so thankful for you all."

"And we are thankful for you, Julie," said Lilly. "Like Barb said, we are all family now, and we are here for you now and anytime down the road you need us."

She patted Julie's shoulder and then walked back to the front of the room. "Shall we get back to today's step?"

The group nodded, and everyone settled back into their seats.

"So we know Julie's story. Being protected with insurance, Julie can concentrate on her grief and her children's grief instead of how they are going to pay for their next meal. That's how important this part of the house is. If you have no roof, one bad storm and every bit of the house is gone."

Lilly drew a lightning bolt above the roof for emphasis.

"Who else has felt their roof tested?" she asked.

My breath caught. Before I could stop myself, my hand rose. "My roof didn't just get tested," I said softly. "It blew right off."

I paused, searching for the words. No one spoke, as though they were holding the silence for me.

"I had it all once," I continued. "A foundation, strong walls, and yes, a roof. Life insurance, critical illness, disability coverage, even policies for the kids. My husband and I thought of everything."

I paused for a moment.

"Well, we thought of protecting ourselves from everything but divorce. Is there insurance for that?" I asked, a smile tugging on my lips.

"I'm surprised that an insurance company hasn't thought of that," Roxanne said, mulling the prospect of it over in her mind.

"Right?" I responded.

"I guess that it would be too expensive of a policy when the odds are stacked against us," Roxanne added.

The group of women all laughed except me.

Roxanne looked at me and lowered her head. "I'm sorry, Zoe," she said, looking back up at me. "I wasn't trying to hurt your feelings."

"I know, Roxanne. I guess I just didn't realize until now that I'm on the wrong side of that statistic."

I felt the weight of that and then shrugged, trying to loosen the grip of failure.

"I think you're on the right side of that statistic, Zoe," Roxanne said quietly. "You're free."

"Yes. I. Am." I smiled at her and then looked over at Lilly, somewhat embarrassed that I had taken over the lesson. "Sorry, Lilly."

"Zoe, you have nothing to be sorry about. You are right, it would be great if there were insurance that protects us through divorce. But well done for the protection you put in place for everything else. Most people are lucky to have life insurance, let alone disability and critical care," Lilly said, trying to encourage me.

"When we separated," I said, "I felt as though I was standing in a storm. I had to untangle it all—what was joint, what was mine, who was paying for what. I had to change beneficiaries, cancel some policies, and keep others. The kids' coverage... I refused to let go of that. I want them to step into adulthood with a safety net I never had."

I had said this in my head a thousand times. This time, I said it out loud, "And the advisor I had was old-school and transactional. He spoke in codes and policy numbers, never once asking me what I wanted my roof to cover—just telling me what he thought was 'enough.' All I wanted to know was: Are the kids and I going to be okay?"

Lilly stepped forward, her voice soft but unshakable. "Zoe, what you're doing is what most people avoid: You are reinforcing your roof so you can live in peace, not worry."

She turned back to the whiteboard and drew three shingles across the roof.

"Think of insurance as three main kinds of protection," she said. "Each one reinforces your ability to move forward with confidence, no matter what life brings."

Lilly rested her hand on the first shingle: *Life Insurance.*

"This one, for some of you, is already very real. Life insurance is what carries your loved ones when you no longer can. It can pay off debts, cover the mortgage, and give your children or family space to grieve without worrying about money. It's the love letter you leave behind. And as we know from Julie's story, the proceeds from life insurance can be what allows a family to keep going in the middle of heartbreak."

Her eyes softened as they met Julie's, the room holding its breath in quiet respect.

Then Lilly tapped the second and third shingles. *Critical Illness* and *Disability.*

"These two are very different. They're not about what happens after you're gone, but about protecting your life while you're still here.

A critical illness payout gives you breathing room if you're diagnosed with something serious, like a heart attack, cancer, or stroke. It allows you the freedom to heal, without worrying about how the bills will get paid.

Disability coverage protects your paycheck. If you cannot work, it keeps the lights on, the fridge full, and your life moving forward. Think of it as ensuring your greatest asset—your ability to earn."

She paused. "And I want to say this especially to the single women in this room. These protections are your lifeline. When there isn't a partner's income to fall back on, critical illness and disability insurance are what stand between you and financial freefall. They are not luxuries—they are your foundation that holds everything in place."

Lilly stepped back, her marker poised.

"Some women only have one of these. Some have all three, like Zoe. There's no one right answer—it depends on your situation, your family, and your values. But the point is, your roof has to fit the house you've built. Too small, and you'll get soaked. Too big, and you'll pay for more coverage than you need. The goal is balance: protection that gives you peace of mind without weighing you down."

I glanced down at my journal. I had sketched the *Wealth Blueprint* on a fresh, new page. For so long, I'd only seen the mess, the policies, the frustration, the endless calls. But as Lilly spoke, something shifted.

I realized that even through the storms, I had what we needed to protect us. I *had* the coverage. Life, critical illness, disability, and insurance for the kids. It hadn't been perfect, but it was there.

For the first time, I let myself feel it: Not the exhaustion of sorting it out, but the relief of knowing I had already given my children and myself solid protection. A roof that, even in pieces, had kept us safe.

A small smile tugged at the corner of my mouth. I decided at that moment to put a heart around the house I had drawn. Maybe I hadn't failed as much as I thought. Maybe, somewhere in those past decisions, I had shown myself more love than I realized.

I sat a little taller in my chair, pen steady in my hand, and wrote:

I am covered. I am protected. I can rebuild from here.

***

To reflect on your own "roof of protection," proceed to page 219.

Chapter 16

The Celebration

Lilly

I walked down to the beach to check on the preparations for our last dinner together to ensure everything was perfect. The scent of grilled lemongrass, sharp and savory, mingled with the salty ocean air, wrapped around us as the sun melted into the horizon in a blaze of color. Tiki torches lined the beach, casting a warm glow and promising an unforgettable night. A long table draped in white linen stretched across the sand, decorated with orchids, golden shells, and flickering tealights. Beside the heavy, gold-rimmed plates, crystal glasses shimmered with reflected light. Soft, cushioned chairs lined the perimeter, and woven lanterns cast a starlight-like glow from above.

The chef and Reagan, clipboard in hand, were deep in conversation. I looked at Reagan and couldn't imagine how I would've managed this week without her support. Having her as my assistant for the last three years has been amazing because her organizational skills and attention to detail mesh so well with my big-picture thinking.

I walked over to her and Chef Guerard. "Everything okay?"

They both looked up at me in unison. "Yes, yes," Chef Guerard answered with his heavy French accent. "Everything is prepared as requested."

"It looks beautiful. Well done to the both of you. You know this is no ordinary dinner—it's a celebration."

"Don't worry, Lilly. I've got it all covered. The champagne is chilled. All the dishes are cooked to perfection, and look at the beautiful tablescape they created." Reagan grabbed Lilly's hand with both of hers. "You did it! Your first small retreat was a success. Shall we have a small toast before the ladies get here?"

Reagan looked over at a waiter standing to the side and nodded. He quickly filled two flutes of champagne and brought them over on a tray. Reagan handed one to Lilly and then took the other one. "This is a celebration dinner, Lilly. Let's first celebrate you. Well done, my friend." And then she clinked her glass to Lilly's.

"This was a group effort. You and Keeley have been working tirelessly to keep this all going. Katie has been amazing with breathwork, meditation and yoga. And every staff member here has gone above and beyond. I am so blessed to have you all on my team."

I pressed the back of my hand to stop a tear from trickling down. "No crying," I said. "Even though they are happy tears."

"Cheers to happy tears," Reagan said, raising her glass and then taking a sip. "Now I have to get back to work. I see our guests are starting to arrive.

I looked up the path where Reagan had been glancing and could see two women in the distance, knowing the others wouldn't be far behind. Barefoot, the women donned silk and linen in vibrant hues, their sun-kissed shoulders gleaming and eyes brighter than I'd witnessed all week.

Before long, we were all seated at the impeccably prepared table, and it truly felt like a celebration. A wave of laughter washed over the group, intermingling with the delicate clink of plates and the effervescent hiss of champagne, as fragrant Balinese dishes made their rounds. Rich coconut curry followed fluffy, yellow saffron rice. Lime-marinated prawns, grilled to perfection, were a sharp contrast to the sweet mango sticky rice. And to match the importance of the night, the chef prepared a special ceremonial dish, babi guling, a roasted suckling pig infused with a rich spice mix that filled the air with mouth-watering aromas.

My eyes swept across the table, amazed that only six days ago, we had been strangers. Now, a deep, unspoken bond connected us in a profound way. This was a group of women bound by poignant, shared experiences that had created a strong and supportive sisterhood.

Just beyond the torches, the soft beat of drums echoed across the beach. A trio of local dancers stepped into the torchlight, their hands fluid, eyes sharp, bodies moving in divine rhythm. The bells on their ankles chimed softly with each step, and I couldn't take my eyes off the graceful dance they performed. The women moved in tune with the music, with huge smiles on their faces.

I watched them for a moment, captivated by the sight.

As the dancers bowed and the final drumbeat faded into silence, the women erupted in enthusiastic applause. Some even whistled and hollered, their joy fizzing and overflowing like the champagne.

As the applause softened, I stood up, feeling my dress swaying in the gentle breeze, and my hair salty and windblown. My heart was wide open, with love and gratitude.

"Ladies," I began, raising my glass. "Tonight means more to me than I can put into words."

As they turned to me, their eyes were glowing with the reflected orange of the torchlight. Some had misty eyes, reflecting a deep well of emotion. Some faces shone, lit up with pure, unfiltered happiness that radiated outward.

"As you know, this was my first small-group retreat," I said, smiling. "And I'll be honest—I was nervous. I've spoken on stages with thousands of people, but going deeper with just eight women? I had no idea how deeply it would affect me. I thought I was coming to *teach*... but to my surprise, I was also the student, learning to go deeper—with myself, and with each of you."

The women nodded, their faces showing both a shared understanding and encouragement for me to continue.

"You showed up fully. You shared your stories with courage and honesty. You let yourselves be seen for who you truly are. And you told your truth, a rare and precious thing, in a world that rewards pretending."

Emotion rose hot in my chest. I paused, drawing in a long, slow breath. A few in the group dabbed their eyes with their napkins.

"So, I want to thank you," I continued. "For your honesty and for choosing to be seen—even when it was terrifying. That kind of vulnerability? That's the real power."

A gentle wind lifted my ruffled hair. The ocean's gentle waves rhythmically lapped at the sandy shoreline. The moon, a massive golden orb, rose silently behind us.

"And... I want to remind you of something I believe deep down in my core: If you wait for perfection to celebrate, you'll miss the genuine joy of the journey. This is the last and most powerful step in this program."

I let the words settle.

"Celebrate now. Celebrate often. Celebrate it all: Past, present, and all the wonderful things coming in the future. Every celebration is a signal to the universe: *More of this, please.* So cheers to more!"

Raising the glass in my hand, I watched as the others mirrored my action, the crystal sparkling in the light. I clinked Sofia's glass, then Mikayla's, as they sat on either side of me. Then, the sound of glass meeting glass, combined with laughter and cheering, stirred a feeling in my heart that I hadn't felt for quite some time. It was pure joy mixed with a deep level of fulfillment.

When the table quieted, I continued. "If you want to manifest your best life, then celebrate even the smallest step. Be grateful for everything—*even the challenges.* They are not obstacles. They are invitations to rise."

I stepped back slightly, hands pressed against my heart.

"So, I want to ask you..." I scanned the table slowly, letting my gaze meet each woman's. "Over the past week, you've given pieces of yourselves, your honesty, your laughter, your tears. You've let yourselves be seen. Tonight, I want to invite you to name just one thing you've accomplished here that deserves to be celebrated. Because if there's one truth I know, it's this: What we honor, we multiply."

There was a moment of awkward silence before Sofia raised her hand, and I nodded for her to share.

She rose with slow, deliberate grace, palms pressing firmly against the table as though grounding herself in the moment. The deep pink of her dress caught the flickering torchlight, shimmering like rose gold as it shifted across the fabric. Her shoulders drew back. Her gaze sharpened. And in that instant, she looked every bit a woman who had found her way back to herself.

"I didn't think I'd ever say this," she said, her voice thick with emotion, "but... I'm learning to love money."

A wave of soft "yeses" rippled through the group, their faces showing support.

Sofia smiled. "No more chasing it or fearing it. I mean, *love* it. I used to think that having money made me greedy, maybe even selfish. But this week, I realized it just means I'm worthy."

She glanced down, then back up.

"I realized I don't have to be ashamed of wanting more. And I don't have to earn my way into worthiness either."

She took a breath.

"I'm working on creating my *Mindful Money Solution*. And for the first time, I'm not scared. I actually think it's going to be easy. Because now I know my purpose."

The group shared smiles and affirming nods.

"When I return home, I'll start saving up my first and last month's rent. I'm ready to move out of my mom's basement. *That* is what I'm celebrating tonight."

Cheers erupted. Dorothy reached over and squeezed her hand. Sofia sat back down, cheeks flushed, but glowing from something deeper than pride.

"That," I said, smiling, "is what it means to embody your wealthy self-image. Not when you have it all—but when you *decide* to live like you're already whole. Well done, Sofia!" I paused before turning back to the group. "Would anyone else like to share?"

Barb raised her hand and then stood, a bit of a nervous smile wavering before she squared her shoulders, taking a deep breath to steady herself.

"Okay," she said, "so this might sound small to some people, but... I finally let myself spend some money. Just for me. Not because I needed it. Not because it was on sale. Not because someone else needed something first. Just... because I wanted it."

She looked over at me before continuing, and I gave her an encouraging smile.

"During the shopping trip," she continued, her voice a little shaky, "I bought a colorful, hand-woven dress. I haven't worn a dress in years—not since we lost the farm. Growing up in a traditional, frugal home, my sister and I wore long, plain dresses our mother stitched from whatever fabric she had. How we dressed was one of the rules we followed without question."

Lori squeezed her hand, encouraging her to continue.

"But when the farm collapsed due to years of bad luck and bad weather, I stopped trusting those rules. No matter how faithful we'd been, and even though we had done everything right, we lost everything. After that, I refused to go back to wearing dresses. I pushed back against the rules around femininity and fashion and started wearing mostly men's style of clothes. It was my way of saying I wouldn't play by their rules anymore."

I watched as a huge smile spread across Barb's face.

"And then I saw this dress, and I thought... maybe it's time. Maybe it's okay to be seen again. To choose softness. When I first came out of the dressing room and looked in the mirror, I was shocked and so uncomfortable."

A few of the women chuckled.

"But looking deeply at my reflection, I saw a strong, resilient woman who had beaten cancer and was ready to embrace all of me, even that little girl who loved twirling in a new dress. When I get home, I'm going to invest in other things that bring me joy. And I've already booked an appointment with a wealth advisor. I want to learn how to invest what I've saved. I want to donate, too—partly for tax purposes, sure, but also because I want to support cancer research—and a cat rescue, too. I love those little furry creatures."

She grinned, and a laugh escaped her.

"And honestly," she added, her voice softening, "I'm so grateful for all of you. You gave me the courage to be seen. And to stop hiding from the joy that friendship might bring into my life. There's a knitting group back home I've wanted to join for years, but I was always too shy. Not anymore. I'm going to sign up."

Barb sat down, cheeks flushed with pride and a hint of disbelief that she had just said all that out loud, as the women clapped loudly. She reached for her water glass with hands that were trembling slightly.

I stepped forward and met her gaze. "Barb," I said, my voice soft and full, "what you just shared was...everything."

She smiled shyly, eyes glossy.

"You did not just buy a gorgeous dress. You said yes to yourself. And then you said yes to building a future that aligns with who you really are—not who you were taught to be. That is not a small win. That is a foundational shift."

I turned slightly to include the rest of the group.

"I hope you all felt that. Barb didn't wait until her entire financial plan was perfect to take action. She didn't wait until she had it all figured out to celebrate. She made one aligned choice and then another. And that is what builds momentum, the kind that shifts your inner frequency and transforms the world around you."

I turned back to Barb.

"And when you join that knitting group... I hope you walk in with your shoulders high and your heart wide open, because they are lucky to have you."

Roxanne shouted, "Way to go, Barb!" and laughter followed.

"Who would like to share next?" I asked, looking around the table.

Mikayla raised her hand.

She didn't stand. Instead, she leaned forward, eyes sparkling, one hand idly circling her wine glass.

"So, I've been doing the work, you know?" she said. "Really feeling into being *worthy*. Not just writing the affirmations and going through the motions. But like... fully embracing what it feels like to be me. I've been journaling about it every morning. Letting go of all these old stories. And learning to listen to my voice, not my father's."

Mikayla had a presence. She always had. But now it was even more powerful.

"Well, this morning," she continued, "after posting a very vulnerable story on Instagram, about being worthy, I checked my phone, and guess what? I had a DM from a woman saying she wanted to work with me. She *found me*. No effort. No pitch. Just... attraction. Her company needs a new branding and marketing strategy.

I already have a million ideas. Also, I make money occasionally as an influencer, and I got an email that a job I did months ago is finally getting paid out... and it's more than I originally thought."

There was a soft ripple of delighted gasps and a few celebratory cheers.

"I swear," Mikayla said, grinning now, "the moment I let go of the unworthiness, something shifted energetically. Like the Universe said, 'Okay, she's ready now.'"

She laughed, glowing.

"I'm one hundred percent celebrating that. Attracting my perfect client, embracing my highest vibration, and living from a place of service. It is a new way for me to show up in the world. And I already decided—I'm putting the income toward my debt."

She leaned back in her chair, eyes shining with something new: certainty.

"And when I get home, I'm selling all the stuff I bought but never used. Some even still have the tags on them. They are all going up on Poshmark. I'd rather have cash to pay my debt and confidence in my financial plan than stuff."

The group clapped again, louder this time. Lori gave her a high-five.

"Oh!" Mikayla added, raising a finger. "And while I was here—I also built my own *Mindful Money Solution*. These tools gave me so much clarity... it all just clicked. And the best thing? I finally let go of the belief that making money has to be hard."

She exhaled a slow, satisfied breath. "Like Sofia mentioned, it gets easier now that I know my purpose."

I stepped toward Mikayla, placing a hand gently on the back of her chair.

"Mikayla," I said, my voice low but sure, "you just spoke the language of abundance. You let go of the story... and the client came. You stopped trying to earn your worth... and started receiving from it. That's the energy that opens doors you do not have to knock on."

She let out a soft giggle.

I leaned in just a little closer, speaking not just to her but to the woman inside her who once thought the price tag defined her value. "You didn't manifest a client. You uncovered the most powerful version of *you*. One who trusts. One who receives. One who does not chase but chooses. That's the power you've had all along. And the fact that you're allocating that money toward your debt?" I said, letting the weight of that land, "that's not just smart. That's sovereignty. And I hope you feel damn proud of yourself tonight."

She nodded slowly, and the group erupted in applause once more—this time with a celebratory whoop from someone down the table. Mikayla covered her heart with her hand and mouthed a quiet, "Thank you."

There it was. The woman who had come in with stilettos and shame, now spoke like a woman who had nothing to prove—and everything to claim.

After the cheers faded, Lori stood. She didn't smile nervously. She stood tall, shoulders back, hands still at her sides, a picture of quiet confidence.

"I'm celebrating the fact that I chose me," she said simply. "These last few days... I've been doing breathwork throughout the day whenever I feel overwhelmed. I've been journaling like my life depended on it. And maybe in some ways—it does. I looked at my book of dreams and possibilities, and I made a list. A *real* list of what I want, knowing I deserve it all."

Her chin lifted slightly. Closing her eyes, she took a deep breath. She opened them and looked around the table.

"And if that list doesn't include Joe..." she paused, steadying herself, "that's okay. I'm ready to stop making myself small to stay in something that doesn't feel like the truth anymore. Even if it means I have to walk away."

The women went silent, supporting her with nods and gentle smiles.

"It's time," Lori said, "for me to take control of my money and my life. Not out of fear. But out of love. For me."

A few women reached for their napkins, dabbing at tears. Roxanne whispered, "Yes, girl."

I felt the weight of Lori's decision—both sacred and liberating.

She slowly lowered herself back down into her seat.

"This," I said, "is the vibration of wealth. It is not about the dollars in your bank account. It is about the decisions you make when you remember who you are. Lori, you are a queen, and so are each and every one of you. You are harnessing the power of your wealthy self-image and remaining strong in your boundaries and standards. You are no longer tolerating anything less."

The flames flickered in agreement.

Mikayla hugged Lori tightly, and Barb grabbed her hand, offering

a reassuring squeeze of support while the other women applaud-
ed.

After the table quieted, Roxanne stood.

"I'm celebrating something simple... but honestly, it's changed
the way I look at everything," she said.

The women turned toward her with warmth and respect.

"I've been getting up early."

A little laughter. A few claps. Lori said, "Yes, girl!"

"Really, I have," she laughed. "I used to think I was a night owl,
and I'd NEVER be one of those 'morning people,' but this week,
I started waking up with the sun—and I *love* it. Now I know to
never say never."

She smoothed her hair, tucking it delicately behind her ear, and
straightened her shoulders with a determined lift. "I've been
stacking my habits. Little by little. Meditation. Journaling. Moving my body. Planning my time so it includes a money date. And
I feel like I finally have some control back. Not over everything,
but over how I *start each day*. And that has changed how I finish
each day."

There were nods all around.

"I'd love to take it even further," she added. "I'm even thinking
about finding an accountability partner."

Before anyone else could speak, Sofia grinned and said, "Pick me.
Pick me!"

Laughter bubbled up from the group.

Roxanne grinned. "Really?"

Sofia nodded. "Absolutely! I'd love to have an accountability partner."

Roxanne looked out at the ocean, her expression shifting to something more resolute.

"And there's something else," she added. "I've decided to stay in Bali. Just for a while. I want to make some money while I'm here, keep stacking those habits—and then…" She paused, a playful light in her eye. "I'm going to Australia."

A few women gasped with surprise.

"I met someone before the retreat. It was very unexpected. But I'm open to the possibility. And I've been doing the work—not just on my mindset, but on my self-image. I want to change how I show up. I finally believe I am worthy of big clients, big opportunities, and big love. And I know I can call them all in. I'll pay for that ticket to Australia to go see him with money I earn from clients who see my value—because now *I* see it too."

The group erupted in cheers.

I smiled at her, filled with the quiet pride that comes from witnessing someone choose their life.

"You don't have to wait for success to feel like a woman in command of her life," I said. "You became her when you said yes to your mornings; yes to being the woman who chooses her path instead of hoping one shows up."

Roxanne nodded, eyes gleaming.

As the chatter from Roxanne's story settled, a quiet shift moved through the group.

Then Julie stood.

Her presence was gentle, steady. Her blue silk dress caught the light, and there was a calm in her eyes I hadn't seen earlier in the week.

"I didn't know if I was going to share tonight," she said softly. "But I think... I think it's time."

The group turned towards her, and Julie took a slow breath.

"When I get back home, I am going to the bank. I am going to pay off the mortgage. And I am also going to hire a wealth advisor. For real this time. Not just another meeting I cancel or reschedule. I have decided to be in command of my money, not afraid of it. I want to know where it's going, and I want it to grow."

She paused, battling the emotion swelling just beneath the surface.

"And... I have also made the decision to sign up to work with Lilly. One-on-one."

I felt a wave of emotion rise in my chest. The entire group turned toward me and then back to her, already clapping.

Julie smiled through a sheen of tears.

"I want to work with Lilly, not just to learn about money, but to reclaim myself. To get my confidence back. To remember that I'm strong. That I'm capable. That I can do this life—and do it well— without Ryan."

A hush settled over the table.

"Being here with all of you... it changed something. You helped me realize I don't have to stay in grief to honor him. I can protect my boys and lead them, not just stay stuck trying to hold it all together."

The applause was soft at first and then grew, raw and heartfelt. I leaned over and gently touched Julie's shoulder.

"You should be so proud of yourself," I said, my voice thick with emotion. "Your boys will see a woman who is brave and strong at the most difficult time in her life. You are an inspiration to them... to all of us."

Julie nodded, wiping a tear from her cheek.

Zoe raised her glass and said, "To Julie." The group clinked glasses and repeated, "To Julie."

And I thought—yes, to Julie.

As the cheers for Julie quieted and a few women wiped away their own tears, Zoe cleared her throat.

She didn't stand. She simply placed her hands gently on the table, fingers brushing the edge of the bottom of her champagne flute.

"Like Lori, I'm celebrating choosing me," she said.

Her gaze dropped for a moment, and then she looked down at her hand. Her ring glinted softly in the candlelight—a smooth larimar stone wrapped in a golden sunburst setting. She held up her hand for all to see.

"I bought this here in Bali," she said. "On our shopping trip, I wandered into a jewelry store. I wasn't even planning to stop, but something drew me inside. When I slid it on my finger... I felt it. The stone, the gold band, it wasn't a decision. It was like it had already been mine. It was waiting for me."

Her thumb stroked the band absently, like it was still sinking in.

"This is a declaration that I'm worthy of everything I want. I don't need permission anymore." She took a deep breath. "I'm letting the trauma of my marriage go. I've carried it long enough. I don't need to keep replaying the story to prove how strong I was to survive it."

She looked up, eyes steadier now, fire behind the softness.

"This ring is a reminder that I will never allow my ex-husband or anyone to take my power away from me. It is a symbol that I am whole, I am powerful and that I am... a damn queen."

The women cheered loudly, and Mikalya said, "Yes, queen!"

I stepped forward and held her gaze.

"You don't just wear queen energy," I said. "You *embody* it. Well done!"

Zoe squared her shoulders and beamed.

Every woman here had walked through something unthinkable. And every single one had walked out the other side, embracing the power they had all along.

As the group quieted again, holding the warmth of Zoe's declaration, Dorothy stood.

"I wasn't sure when I arrived in Bali that I'd have anything to celebrate tonight," she began, her voice steady but soft, "but... I do."

The women turned toward her with gentle curiosity.

"I had a conversation with my husband yesterday," she said. "A *real* one. Not about the kids or the bills. We had a conversation about us."

She paused, her face betraying the complex emotions within.

"I told him everything I was feeling. I told him about all I've learned here and how it has changed me. How I want to take more ownership of our finances. About how disconnected I've felt from myself, our money, and him. And to my surprise," Dorothy said, smiling now, "he didn't push back. He didn't get defensive. He listened and said, 'I've missed you, too. I want us to be partners again—in *every way.*'"

There was a collective intake of breath. A few hands pressed over hearts, mine included.

"We've drifted in our marriage. I thought maybe that was just the way it was. But now... he's excited. *I'm* excited. We're going to meet with our wealth advisor when I get back—*together*. And it finally feels like we're on the same team again."

Tears shimmered in her eyes now, but she didn't blink them back.

"Oh—and I also texted my girlfriends," she added with a small, giddy grin. "Told them we need a weekend getaway. They were all in. We're already planning ideas of where to go. I never thought you could have a strong partnership with a spouse and have time for friends. I was so resentful of the time he spent with his. Now I see it makes life fuller for everyone. You are all a great example of that."

The group broke into delighted laughter and applause. Dorothy sat back down, radiant.

"Dorothy," I said, "what you did was incredibly brave. You led with truth.

You opened the door for real connection—not just with your husband, but with yourself."

She nodded and said, "Thanks, Lilly."

"If it helps," I added, "I have a tool I love giving to couples—or anyone trying to rebuild a healthier relationship with money. It's called *Conscious Conversation Starters Around Money*. It includes ten heart-opening questions to invite new conversations about money, worth, and shared vision. Not budgeting. Not blaming. Just soft, honest openings."

Her eyes lit up.

"I'll send them to you," I said. "And maybe you can use one over coffee with your husband. Or even on your girlfriend getaway. We need to take the stigma out of talking about money."

"I'd love that," she said.

And in that moment, under a sky full of stars and with women full of fire, I knew this wasn't just a retreat. It was a revolution.

I stood there watching them, their joy, their vulnerability, their fierce softness and thought: *This is the deep work I want to do.*

I raised my glass once more.

"To bold hearts, brave truths, and the beauty of becoming."

They raised theirs with me.

"To more of this, please!" I said.

"To more of this, please!" they echoed back.

And beneath the stars, with waves kissing the shore and firelight dancing in our eyes, I knew it: We were already wealthy in all the ways that mattered.

***

Later that evening, I stood on the balcony of my villa, arms wrapped around my waist, staring into the dark, endless water.

The women had drifted to bed, full of saffron rice and champagne and something even deeper: a love for themselves.

And me? I had never felt so full. Not even after the big stages, seven-figure launches or hitting the bestsellers' lists. This was different. This was soul-satisfaction.

I closed my eyes, letting the breeze kiss my cheeks. I didn't want the moment to end.

Then my phone pinged.

I opened my eyes, surprised to find I had brought it out with me. Habit, I supposed. I tapped the screen.

Haley

Hey Lilly! Just checking in to see how the retreat went. I'm sure you rocked it! Can't wait to hear all about it and see what your next steps are. Xo
– Haley

I smiled. Haley has been my mindset coach for almost six years now. Proof that no matter how far you go, there's always somewhere deeper to grow. She reminds me who I am when I forget.

I was about to text her back when another message came through.

Oh yeah. Remember that film producer I told you about? I sent her your book. She's interested in shopping it around!!! WOOHOO! Let's go!

I blinked. I was so shocked, I nearly dropped my phone onto the stone tiles below.

My heart raced, but not in a nervous way. In that *of-course-this-is-happening* kind of way. The kind that happens when you are fully aligned with your calling and the Universe is keeping pace.

I exhaled. And I smiled. A slow, knowing smile.

Then I whispered to the waves: "Yes, more of this, please!"

***

Interested in creating your own queen's toast?
You will find more on page 221.

Chapter 17

Final Climb

Zoe

My alarm startled me at two-thirty a.m. I lay still, hand on my chest, and listened as my heartbeat settled back into its normal rhythm. What startled me even more was the fact that I had been sleeping—truly sleeping. A real sleep, the kind I hadn't felt since my divorce.

Before now, my nights had been long stretches of numbing. Netflix playing until the early hours, a bottle of wine drained without thought, my fingers scrolling endlessly through TikTok and Instagram, comparing my unraveling life to the happy highlight reels of strangers. Four hours later, I'd bolt upright, panic gripping my lungs. But not tonight. Tonight, my body had actually rested. That felt like a small, private miracle.

Lilly's session with Roxanne about habits cracked something open in me. Her words looped in my head ever since. How do I see her, the me I want to be? Similar to Roxanne, I had laughed at the idea that I could be a morning person, which was never a part of my DNA. The next night, I went to bed early without bargaining with myself about Netflix and read a chapter of *Eat, Pray, Love*. I woke up to my alarm with the book on my chest.

Today was an even earlier wake-up call. And I am really excited about it.

What surprised me most was that this early morning habit didn't arrive by force. It came on the back of this new, but strange desire to do and be better. I tried to stick to a good routine in the morning and wondered why it never stuck. It wasn't my mornings that were broken—it was my nights.

Staying up late with a glass that became a bottle meant the next day was already decided: sleep through the first alarm, wake groggy and behind, chug coffee to kick-start the day, rush through the kitchen, snap at the kids, apologize in the car, and sprint into work already late. That was the loop.

Now, I am ending my day with the intention to set my morning up for success.

The shower came alive in the outdoor bath, and water poured from the rain head in a warm sheet. Even though I was totally embracing the early morning start, I needed this to wake myself up and get motivated.

Moonlight washed across the parts of me that I have hated to look at. Bare to the sky, I felt exposed yet held. I pressed my palms to my warm skin and breathed with the cadence we had practiced each morning.

It's okay. Breathe. You are going to be okay. Breathe. Let go of who you were. Breathe in who you're becoming.

I felt the words travel, not just as thoughts, but as sensations. With every inhale, my shoulders dropped; with every exhale, I returned to the body I had been abandoning for too long. I am beginning to believe and trust that I am going to be okay.

By the time I was dressed for this morning's hike, I felt lighter, almost giddy. Here I was, up before dawn. I did a quick journal entry, spent one minute envisioning the new me, and set the intention of enjoying every step of this hike, whether my body was protesting the climb or not. Habit stacking works.

And then, standing there in the predawn hush, I felt it hit—a warm, fulfilling wave of gratitude tipping through me, head to toe. *Look at your life*, I told myself. *You are here. You made it here. Your soul asked for this, and you answered.* Tears came, not from sadness, but from the deep knowing that I was meant to be here, in this place, at this exact moment.

The group met out in front of the hotel thirty minutes later. We folded ourselves inside a white minivan, thigh to thigh, shoulder to shoulder. I felt the kind of closeness that would feel awkward with strangers but felt natural here. It *felt* like home, a home where you are fully seen.

Over these past few days, we had sobbed into each other's shoulders without apology, said out loud the secrets we thought would swallow us, and were met with nods instead of fixes. We traded numbers and quiet vows: *Text me anytime. Call when it's messy, and I will answer.* My nervous system, wired for years to scan for danger, finally exhaled. I realized I wasn't alone anymore. I was supported in a way I never had, not by family, not by anyone.

The road climbed into the darkness while the headlights carved a narrow tunnel through ferns and tree trunks. Switchbacks pressed us hip to hip. The van's shocks complained over potholes, gravel pinged the undercarriage, and every bump coaxed a sleepy laugh. We rode in calm silence, sleepy-eyed, saving our words for the mountain.

The road ended at a tiny house clinging to the edge of a cliff. Inside the covered courtyard, a long table waited with tiny cups of strong coffee and a neat stack of Beng-Beng chocolate bars—breakfast of champions for a hike up the mountain. With steam rising from the cups and chocolate sweetness on our tongues, we grinned at each other like kids.

After finishing our breakfast, we were each given a flashlight and a walking stick that resembled a broom pole. Then we stepped into the darkness. The first stretch was flat; my beam of light exposed crops planted neatly along a stone wall adorned with mini statues.

Ketut, our fearless leader, kept a pace quick enough to promise we'd make the summit before six a.m. I watched Mikayla and Sofia fall in behind him, their steps in synchrony with the way their laughter had been since Day One. I drifted to the back and found myself walking alongside Lilly. It was the first time we'd been alone together since I arrived in Bali. Lilly—the woman the internet calls a money goddess—moving beside me under the stars felt surreal.

"Lilly, can I ask you something?" I said.

"Sure, you can always ask me anything."

"What did you have to let go of to become who you are today?"

"That is a great question, Zoe." She paused. "I feel there were three things I had to let go of: Control. Doing everything myself. And the *shoulds*. With control, I stopped forcing outcomes and started listening to my intuition, trusting that it would work out the way it was supposed to. Then I quit using exhaustion as proof of my success and started hiring people to support me. Delegation is a beautiful thing, especially when you have people like Keeley and Reagan on your team. And *should*... well, I retired that word. I now say, *'I want, I choose, and yes, more please.'*"

I nodded and let that settle.

"Do you see yourself in any of those three?" Lilly asked.

I wasn't expecting that question and I hesitated in answering, but soon said, "Of course—actually, every single one. I do everything at home, I control at work, and I have *shoulds* written all over my calendar."

Lilly blurted out a giggle, "Oh yes, that was me one thousand percent. When I'd had enough and was ready to surrender, I started to look at my life like a scientist and ask, 'Is this task, habit, or thought getting me closer to my purpose?' If the answer was no, I gave it away or stopped doing it and shifted my focus to what gave me joy in my life."

"That seems so simple," I said.

"It really is that simple, Zoe. You just have to be persistent and keep your purpose right in front of you at all times. There are no days off alignment. You have to harness your queen energy for you and no one else."

The path narrowed into a single file. I noticed the earth changed beneath my feet, dirt giving way to powdered ash and small rocks that felt like walking on marbles and then to loose volcanic scree.

Heavy breathing replaced giggles and conversation. The slope in front of us tilted just enough to make me pay attention. An hour in, it hit me that this "piece of cake climb" was going to be more than I had bargained for. The burn arrived, first in my calves, then in my quads, both screaming at me to stop. My breath started to become louder. I huffed for air. This is way more challenging than I'd expected. I've completed multiple half marathons. *How can this be so grueling?* I thought.

I was concentrating so hard on placing one foot in front of the other that I didn't see Barb over on the side of me, sitting on a rock, trying to catch her breath. I heard Julie ask if she was okay, and Barb gave a thumbs-up. "I just need a break, but I'll be fine. Chemo treatments were way worse than this."

It got steeper and steeper. The scree was treacherous, and when I slipped, the sharp rocks tore the skin from my palm. I stood. Then I slipped again. Every part of me wanted to turn around.

What the fuck am I doing here?

This isn't what I expected. I can't do this. My breathing was rapid, and I felt dizzy. My feet throbbed, and I couldn't see a thing.

I stopped. Tears welled up in my eyes. I heard footsteps and saw that Barb had caught up to me. She gently placed her hand between my shoulder blades and said in a strong but gentle voice, "Zoe, if I can do this, so can you. Keep breathing and keep moving."

"I know this is tough, Zoe." Lilly's voice emerged out of the darkness. "You are doing amazing. Just remember, you have the power to choose. Do you want to stay here, go back down, or keep moving to catch the dawn of this new day? Only you can decide what it's going to be for you."

I took a deep breath and then thought, *Fuck this. I can do this. I've done harder things. My kids need a mother who doesn't quit. I need to be strong for them. And I need to be strong for me.*

"I'm going to finish this," I said to Lilly. Then I turned to Barb, "Let's go."

That determination fueled the last part of the climb. When I reached the summit, my body was exhausted, but my soul was ecstatic. Gathered a few feet away from the trail were the rest of the ladies, clapping and cheering me, Barb, and Lilly on as we were the last of the group to arrive. They all gathered around me, forming the most comforting group hug I've ever experienced. We held each other tightly, we laughed, we cried, and we hollered that we did it... together!

As we found our way to a wooden bench built along the mountain rock, I could hear Mikalya, Sofia, and Roxanne giggling over how their brand-new pairs of Nike Air Force's went from white to brown and how it really didn't matter.

A hand touched my left knee. It was Julie. "I am really proud of you, Zoe. I heard you stopped along the way and didn't want to continue, but here you are. I wanted to stop so many times as well, but all I could hear was Ryan's voice telling me how proud my kids would be, and that was enough to keep me moving."

I lay my head on her shoulder, "My children were my motivation, too."

I took a deep breath and realized at that moment I knew I was going to be okay.

Minutes later, our guide appeared with a pink plastic tray loaded with oranges, apples, more Beng-Beng chocolate bars, and warm egg salad sandwiches made from cooking the eggs in the volcano's steam. I felt like I had died and gone to heaven. Fueling my empty stomach, I watched as the black sky changed from indigo to inky blue to pink and orange. I was grateful for the opportunity to stand at the top of an ancient volcano and watch the sun come up over the sea.

On the other side of me was Dorothy, and beside her, Lori. In unison, they said, voices filled with awe, "This is the most beautiful sight that I have ever seen." We all started to laugh, as we all felt the same way.

Lilly stepped forward, cheeks pink, and calm as always. "Ladies, I am so proud of you for climbing this volcano before dawn. It has been amazing to see all of you push past your fears and worries to experience this. A sunrise, to me, represents a new day. What happened yesterday is done and over. So let's enjoy the present… it is a gift after all." She smiled and winked.

"Keeley, can I have the envelopes, please?" Keeley walked over to her and pulled a stack of envelopes from her cross-body bag.

"I have written a personal note to each and every one of you. Read it when you are ready. While you take your time to enjoy this moment, I would also like you to remember the intention you all wrote down for this retreat and reflect and compare where you are right now. Then, set your intentions for your return home. Take your time, there is no rush, and we can stay up here as long as you need."

I immediately opened my journal to the first page.

Day One
My intention: To find out who I truly am. I feel lost and helpless about how I will be able to provide for me and my children.

Reading that now feels like a stranger's words and feelings. That version of me, the one who wrote the word "lost," had stayed at the bottom of the mountain. Up here, there is a new me ready to transform.

I thought about the past week. The eight-step journey that Lilly took us on wasn't boxes to check off; each step is a way of living, building and strengthening who I am becoming. I have learned:

That money is a tool. For years, I treated money like it was something to stay far away from for fear of being greedy. I have decided that money is a tool, and when I give it a purpose, it guides me.

To shift my money mindset. I had carried beliefs that weighed me down like a backpack of rocks and kept me stuck: *I'm bad with money. You have to work hard to make money. People like me don't get ahead.* Scarcity has kept me safe and small. Abundance makes everything possible.

To build a wealthy self-image. I know who I need to be to have what I desire in life show up. I give myself permission to embody that feeling now.

To create a vision of prosperity. My vision is not fantasy—it is my future reality waiting for me to step inside. This vision tells my money where to go. If I can see it in my mind, I can hold it in my hands.

About the lifetime habits of prosperity. A life that you desire is built with one domino habit. When you stack one positive habit with another, not only does it change your internal self, but it also reflects out to your external world.

The Mindful Money Solution. For years, my money slipped through my fingers like water. Now it has a purpose—vacation, renovations, prosperity cushion, and giving. Never forget to date it!

The Wealth Blueprint. A plan is scaffolding—the structure that lets me climb higher without clinging in fear. I want nothing more than to build a strong financial house and be a great example to my children.

To celebrate with gratitude. Celebrate each moment not because you must, but because you get to. Gratitude is more than a list—it's a way of metabolizing what's hard. The power is in thanking the messy middle as well.

I let my hand rest over my chest and felt the heat of my palm. I had been chasing other people's stories for most of my life. I wrote down these words to mark this moment:

I matter
I am wealthy
I am divine
I am a queen.

The sun lifted clean over the horizon. Down in the valley, the old story of me being the victim of the affair and the nights crying for hours are both done. None of it defines me now. If he hadn't strayed, I would not be here now. If my life hadn't been shattered, I would never have had the chance to enjoy this feeling of being whole.

I slid a finger under the flap of the envelope and pulled out a card. It read: *You did not come here to be saved, Zoe. You came here to remember who you are. Listen to your inner voice—it always knows the way.*

I turned back to the view and thought about what I wanted to carry home with me.

I wrote in my journal:

I'm bringing with me:

Stacking habits that start my day off right.
An abundant self-image that makes me brave and brings me joy.
Money tools to make wealth a reality.
A sisterhood that I can rely on to keep me on track, cheer me on, and help me when I need it.

A belief in myself that I can do anything.

My attention was stolen by the breathtaking display of colors the sunrise painted across the sky. Before me, I sensed life's infinite possibilities, like a field of flowers waiting to be picked. I made it up this mountain and now know that anything is possible. And this new radiant, resilient, and powerful version of me is ready to experience all of it.

I lifted my face to the sun, let the warmth wash over me, and whispered a quiet thank you to the mountain, to the women who believed in me, and to every heartbreak that broke me open. So many wonderful and horrible things have led me here. I'm thankful for them all.

My thoughts were interrupted when Lilly asked us if we were all ready to go.

I took one last long look at the sky before me and then down to the village below. I slipped the envelope into my pocket, squared my shoulders, and began the descent towards a fresh start and my dream life.

***

Let's honor the truth of who you are. Reflection is found on page 223.

EMBODIMENT SECTION

Chapter Complementary Pages

Chapter 1

Reflection Exercise: The Courage Inventory

I invite you to pause.

You've just met Zoe at a crossroads—not yet healed, not yet whole, but willing to board the plane. Maybe you see pieces of yourself in her heartbreak, her numbness, or her quiet bravery.

This chapter isn't just a story—it's a mirror. It's a chance to notice where *you* might be whispering for change.

You may not feel strong yet. That's okay. Courage often speaks in a whisper rather than a roar.

Write down a moment in your life where you took action even though you were scared. Big or small—it counts.

Then answer:

1. What did I learn about myself?

2. What was the outcome?

3. What *new identity* emerged from that moment?

"Courage is not the absence of fear, but rather the assessment that something else is more important than fear."

~ Franklin D. Roosevelt

Chapter 2

Action Step: You're Worthy of Receiving

Zoe stepped into luxury and peace, but not without fear or guilt. She did it anyway. Now, it's your turn to practice receiving something beautiful—without apology.

1. Choose one thing that feels slightly indulgent, life-enhancing, or joyful: Something you may have once told yourself you did not deserve or could not have. (e.g., a solo lunch at my favorite café, a morning off, silk pajamas, help from someone, a coaching session, new flowers for my space)

I will receive: _____

2. When will you allow yourself to receive it?

Pick a date—make it real.

I will receive this by: _____

3. *What story might try to stop you, and what will you say back?*

Anticipate resistance... Guilt... The inner voice that says not now, not you.

Then choose a new belief.

The old story is: _____

My new belief is: _____

Chapter 3

Mini Challenge: Your Prosperous Self Postcard

You've just taken your first step through the doorway to celebrate your most authentic self. Now it's time to share with the universe and let go of the old story, situation, or belief you once had about yourself and walk through the doorway of prosperity.

Write down three words that describe the most authentic version of yourself. Let your heart answer, not your head.

Open with: Your name: _____

I am so proud of you for becoming your prosperous self. You are:

1.

2.

3.

Chapter 4

The Mirror of Admiration

Sometimes, the people we judge at first glance are the ones who hold the greatest mirror for our own growth.

Maybe you've made assumptions about someone, or dismissed that person, only to realize they embodied a quality you deeply admire—or long to nurture in yourself.

Let's gently explore that.

Think of one person you once misjudged but came to admire or understand more deeply over time.

This could be someone you know well, a public figure, or someone at your workplace.

For this person, reflect on these prompts:

- What did I assume about them at first?

- What truth surprised me once I got to know their story?

- What do I now admire or respect about this person?

- How did this shift affect the way I see myself?

Chapter 5

Exercise: Define Your Financial Purpose

Your financial purpose is not a number, and money is not the goal. It is the life you want money to help you create. It's about who you want to become, how you want to feel, and what you want to experience, give, or build. Take a moment and ask yourself:

What is my financial purpose? Is it...

- To be free from a 9-to-5 job?
- To create security for your future family?
- To experience joy, beauty, or independence?
- To travel or take time off every summer?
- To make an impact and help others rise?

There's no right or wrong answer—just your truth. Write one sentence that feels true and powerful for you. Let that be your anchor, your lens through which you make all future decisions—your "why."

"Money is a tool. It will take you where you wish, but it will not replace you as the driver."

~ Ayn Rand

Chapter 6

Journal Prompt: What Do I Really Believe?

As Lilly says, "Our thoughts, often unconscious, create our feelings. Those feelings drive our actions, and the actions create our results. So, you need to figure out the underlying thoughts before you can change any actions that determine your world."

Knowing this, write freely in response to these questions: (e.g., "I have to work hard to earn money." –> This was what my mother taught me –> "Money can come with ease and joy when I am aligned.")

What is one belief I've carried about money that may no longer be serving me?

Where did this belief come from, and what would I like to believe instead?

Chapter 7

Rewrite Your Self-Image Script

Your self-image is the story you tell yourself about who you are and what you believe you deserve.

This exercise invites you to rewrite that story, not based on your past or your fears, but on who you're becoming.

You don't have to earn your worth; you just have to embody it.

Rewrite Your Self-Image Script: Model / Template

1. Find a quiet spot. Close your eyes, take three deep breaths. Center into your body.

2. Visualize your "wealthy self"—the version of you who already knows she's worthy. How do you walk into a room? What are you wearing? How does this make you feel?

3. Write out a script/declaration of that wealthy self you just visualized in the present tense, including sensory and emotional detail.

4. Include any positive statements, affirmations or truths that you want to live by. For example:

    o "I attract wealth and kindness"

    o "I love money and money loves me."

5. Record your wealthy self-image script on any type of voice recorder. Listen to your new script daily—morning, evening, or when you see yourself in the mirror. Let the feelings align with the words.

For an immersive journey, listen to the guided audio. To download, visit FrancescaRea.com.

This gentle visualization helps you embody your wealthy self-image and anchor into that energy daily.

Chapter 8

Create Your Own Luxury Shopping Experience

As Lilly explained to everyone at the retreat, "This isn't about spending money. This exercise is about stepping into that self-image you created earlier. It is about confronting your money habits and behaviors, pushing you past your subconscious and conscious limitations. It is time to face your feelings of guilt, shame, and low self-worth by observing how you actually restrict yourself or spend money. You are not buying an item today; you are meeting a part of yourself: The one who believes she is allowed to receive."

With this advice, create your own Luxury Shopping Experience. In the moment, take inventory of what you hear, see, taste, touch, or smell.

Here are some examples for you to try on:

- Have tea or coffee at a luxury hotel

- Visit high-end stores to get a feel for what sparks your interest

- Buy flowers for yourself

- Bathe in beautiful, scented bubble bath

- Get your nails done

- Visit a hair salon and get a blowout

- Wear your favorite perfume or lipstick just for fun!

Chapter 9

Create Your Own Vision Board

We all carry a vision, quiet or bold, for the life we deeply desire. Now it's your turn, your opportunity to begin creating a visual reminder of your financial purpose—not just what you want to buy, but what you want to feel, build, and become.

This board is not about perfection. It's not about looking rich or manifesting luxury for the sake of it. It's about clarity. Direction.

Here's how to begin:

1. Choose your platform: Pinterest, Canva, a physical vision board, or even a folder of saved images on your phone.

2. Give your board a meaningful title, for example, *My Abundant Life*, *Be Her*, or *The Life I'm Building*.

3. Start collecting images that reflect:

- How you want to *feel* (free, peaceful, joyful, worthy, relaxed)

- What you want to *experience* (connection, travel, creative work, love, giving back)

- Spaces, people, textures, colors, moments that reflect you and your life built on purpose

4. Try to include at least one image that feels symbolic of the impact you want to make or the legacy you want to leave.

5. When your board feels complete (or close enough), take a moment to reflect on this:

How can I begin using money as a tool to build this life, one aligned decision at a time?

You don't need to wait for "someday." You can start now. Even the smallest aligned action can become the foundation of your *Divine Wealth*.

Chapter 10

Discovering Your Queen Energy

Your queen energy isn't somewhere outside of you. It already lives within you, waiting to be remembered and expressed. Try one (or all) of these practices and notice which awakens your inner queen most naturally.

Ways You Might Tap Into Your Queen Energy

- Stand or walk tall

- Put on clothes that make you feel radiant and powerful

- Sit with your favorite candle or scent and simply be

- Move your body to awaken your energy

- Rest fully—pause, receive, and let your queen self draw in strength

- Put on music that ignites your queen spirit

My crown is always with me, but music has a way of amplifying that energy. These songs remind me of my strength, my radiance, and my power in who I am. I've gathered them into a Spotify playlist so you can feel that rise, too.

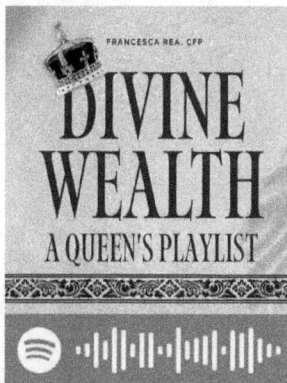

FRANCESCA REA, CFP

DIVINE WEALTH
A QUEEN'S PLAYLIST

Chapter 11

Mini Exercise: Create Your Domino Habit

Self-help author Bob Proctor believed that transformation doesn't happen through a massive overhaul, but rather through small, consistent shifts. You don't need to change everything. In fact, trying to do that often leads to burnout and disappointment.

What you *can* do is start with one habit—one small, intentional act that creates momentum. With having your financial purpose in mind as your guide, choose one small, doable habit that could become your anchor—your first domino.

It might be:

- Waking up 30 minutes earlier than you typically do now
- Tracking your expenses three times a week
- A five-minute guided meditation in the morning
- Laying out your clothes the night before

Now answer:

- What time of day will I do this?

- What existing routine can I stack it onto? (e.g., "After brushing my teeth, I will…")

Chapter 12

Daily Gratitude Ritual

Gratitude involves showing appreciation for the things in life that are meaningful or valuable to you. I believe it's also important to give thanks to those not-so-great moments or people in your life that helped you to grow. Research has shown that daily gratitude for everything in life can have multiple positive effects, such as a brighter outlook, a boost in mood, better sleep, and increased self-esteem and patience.

For this exercise, I would like you to consider one moment in time or a person who didn't seem "worthy" of gratitude. Maybe it was a hard conversation, a moment of discomfort, or an old trigger. Sit with it for a moment and then ask:

- What did this moment show me?

- What part of me is healing or growing through this?

- Can I thank it, even just a little?

Whisper it if you need to: *Thank the mess. Thank the magic. Thank it all.*

Chapter 13

Create Your Mindful Money Solution

"Where your money goes, your power grows."

You've already done the beautiful work of identifying your financial purpose back in Chapter 5. Now it's time to take that purpose and bring it to life—not just as a concept, but as a *real, tangible system* that supports you with clarity, ease, and joy.

Step 1: Write it down again here, to bring it forward:

My current financial purpose is:

_____

Step 2: Now ask yourself: *For me, this purpose would include...* and then name one specific thing that brings this purpose to life (e.g., *travel, donate more to charity, or save for my children's education*).

_____

_____

Step 3: Open a Purpose Savings Account just for this dream. Give it a name that reflects your intention—something joyful, not generic. Estimate what it would cost to fund this purpose.

Estimated total cost: $_____

Goal date (how many months away?): _____

Monthly savings needed: $_____

Biweekly (optional): $_____

Step 4: Set up automatic transfers from your main income account. Every time you get paid, this amount goes into your Purpose Savings Account *before* anything else. No thinking, no guilt, no stress—just alignment.

Step 5: Anchor it with intention. Before the money leaves your account, take a breath and say:

> *This is me choosing my future on purpose.*
>
> *I'm not spending, I'm building a life I love.*

Chapter 14

Reflection Exercise: Wealth Blueprint

- Where in your financial house do you not have peace of mind?

- What are the steps you would like to take to bring peace of mind to those areas?

- Put a heart near the ones you feel you have taken care of.

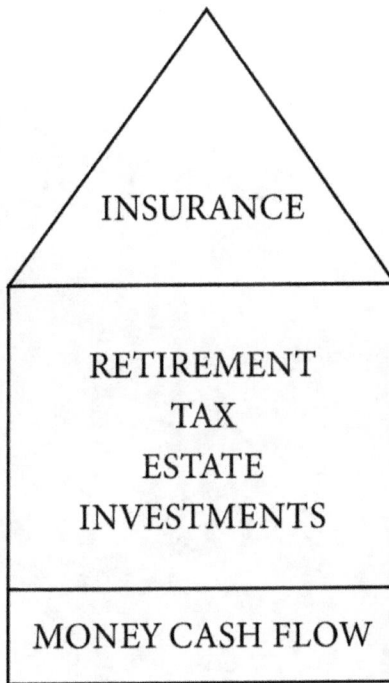

INSURANCE

RETIREMENT
TAX
ESTATE
INVESTMENTS

MONEY CASH FLOW

_____

_____

_____

Chapter 15

Journal Prompt: Protecting What You Have

At the retreat, Zoe realized that insurance isn't just paperwork—it's love made practical. It's the roof that shields everything you've built. This reflection will help you look at your own "roof of protection" with both imagination and intention.

You are your greatest asset. Your ability to earn, create, and contribute is what makes your wealth blueprint possible in the first place.

Reflect and journal about one or two steps you've already taken (or want to take) to protect your income, your well-being, and those that you love.

Chapter 16

Create Your "Queen's Toast"

Celebration isn't just about the big moments—it's about honoring the steps along the way. In our busy lives, we often rush from one goal to the next, forgetting that *celebration is a practice of presence*. It's how we build an *attitude of gratitude*, not just for what we've achieved, but for the journey that got us there.

When we take a moment to acknowledge our progress—big or small—we're placing a bookmark in the story of our lives. These small celebrations become milestones, reminding us not only of what we've accomplished but who we are becoming along the way.

Write a short toast to yourself, as if you were at the Bali retreat table. Write out as many items as you wish to celebrate. Raise your imaginary glass and finish the sentence:

I'm celebrating...

Then follow it with one of the most powerful affirmations:

Yes, more of this please.

Say it out loud if you can. You deserve to be witnessed—even by yourself.

Chapter 17

Reflection: Letting Go

As you finish this journey, take a quiet moment to pause and honor where you are.

What one thing (habits, thoughts, or "shoulds") are you ready to release, just as Zoe did on her climb?

Now, set an intention for what comes next—for the life you will step into after turning the last page of this book.

Read that intention and breathe in the truth of who you are and repeat these words aloud or silently:

I matter.

I am wealthy.

I am divine.

I am a queen.

Acknowledgments

It all began with the word "sabotage." I was listening to a free mindset masterclass when a woman named Adele Tevlin said something that hit me hard: "We, as women, sabotage ourselves because we don't think we're worthy." Earlier that morning, I had told a friend I wasn't "worthy" to spend time with someone (who shall remain unnamed). In that moment, I realized I was the *queen* of self-sabotage, yet I knew I was meant for more. Why do I believe I am not worthy? It was divine timing that I met Adele, and so began my journey. I was hooked. Changing my thinking became the only way I could survive my separation and divorce.

After Adele, the next mentor to enter my life was Danielle Amos—the Mystic Millionaire Mentor. Working with Danielle through her *Mystic Millionaire Method* cracked something open in me. Alongside Bob Proctor's teachings, she helped me rebuild my self-image from the inside out. She saw me like no one ever had before. It was after attending her VIP day that everything shifted and the *quantum leap* began.

Danielle, I dedicate the *Wealthy Self-Image* and *Luxury Shopping Experience* steps of my work to you. You were the inspiration behind them. I still use your tools daily—self-image scripting, visualization, and surrounding myself with joy. Thank you for the leap. You are the real deal. Never stop shining your light.

This year—2025—was all about energy. Thank you to Elvira Hopper and Haley Bowler-Cooke for helping me remember that my energy is everything. Both of you encouraged me that it's time to wear the crown. And yes, there were days when I forgot. But then I hear Haley's voice in my head whispering, "No days off," and I get back up—head high, crown on, energy realigned. I am grateful to both of you for entering into my life.

This book, *Divine Wealth*, would not exist without my incredible book team. First, to Darlene Gudrie Butts, my brilliant book coach. Divine timing brought us together on that fateful August evening in 2024. I had set an intention to meet someone who would help me get on stages—and the universe delivered you. Your wisdom, your patience with my endless Voxer notes, and your unwavering belief in this book kept me going. You truly do lead "women to create their soul-level healing by reconnecting with their magic." Thank you for helping me bring mine to life.

To my behind-the-scenes dream team. Anna Fillapone, my hilarious editor—thank you for turning my chaos into clarity and for making me laugh in the process. Jennifer Traynor, your meticulous proof-reading and formatting magic made the final manuscript shine. Lastly, thank you, Heather Andrews, for guiding me through the wild world of self-publishing with such ease and confidence. You three made this journey not only possible but enjoyable.

To the brilliant team at Media Vandals, thank you for bringing my vision to life with your creativity, wit, and lightning-fast brilliance. From the book cover to my branding, website, and socials, you captured the essence of *Divine Wealth* in a way that was both fun and exciting. Working with you has been an absolute joy.

To my beta readers, you know who you are. I'll be honest: sharing this story with you scared me. You all knew parts of my *real* story, and I worried you might not love the fictional version. But your encouragement, insights, and heartfelt words lit a fire in me, and a huge sense of confidence in myself. You made me believe I could truly call myself an author. Thank you for taking the time to read my work with such open hearts and honest eyes. Your encouragement and insights gave me the confidence to share it with the world. It gave me the push I needed to finish strong.

To Ellen Rogin, thank you for being a guiding light in the space where money meets mindset. As a money expert and financial intuitive, your wisdom affirmed that wealth management and purpose truly belong together—and I'm deeply grateful for your generous testimonial and early support of *Divine Wealth*.

To my parents, Paul and Donna, thank you for, well… making me! Your constant love, support and patience with my lifelong need to be in the spotlight have shaped who I am. Thank you for showing me what love, resilience, and family truly mean. Everything I am is because of the foundation you built.

To Mike, my adventurous partner—thank you for never wavering in your support. You gave me space when I needed to write, hugs when I wanted to quit, and kisses when my brain turned to mush. Thank you for letting me be me. I cannot wait for all the chapters we will write together on and off the page.

I do want to express gratitude to my ex-husband. Thank you for being part of my story and for giving me our two beautiful children, Keeler and Aidan—the greatest gifts of my life. You two are my everything—my why, my purpose. Never give up on your dreams, no matter what life throws at you. You have the power to create the life you want. And remember, I will always be cheering you on every step of the way.

And to all those people who said I couldn't have this book ready by November 18, 2025, thank you. You gave me the fire to prove that I could. I pinned the date and never wavered. The old me would have believed the doubts of others; the new me had trust, faith, focus, and sheer determination to reach the finish line.

Lastly, a big thank you to Bob Proctor, and his saying, "If you can see it in your mind, you can hold it in your hand." I repeated this over and over in my mind when I was ready to give up.

In my final parting words: If you're holding a vision right now, don't let it go. Keep the faith. Keep going. And trust that it is for you to have. Never forget:

I matter.
I am wealthy.
I am divine.
I am a Queen.

About the Author

Francesca Rea, CFP®, is redefining what it means to be a wealth advisor. As an educator, speaker, and now author, she integrates the mindset and beliefs we hold around money into traditional wealth management—empowering women of all ages and stages of life to not only build net worth, but also inner confidence and clarity about their financial future.

Her own journey provides both inspiration and credibility. Once a debt-burdened student juggling credit cards and personal loans, Francesca became a proud homeowner, business owner, and single mother who turned life's obstacles into stepping stones. Having lived the financial curveballs life can throw, she brings clients more than expertise; she brings empathy forged through experience.

A Certified Financial Planner (CFP®), Francesca has mastered the disciplines of investing, tax-efficient planning, wealth growth and preservation, and knows financial success begins with mindset. Her holistic approach helps clients align their beliefs about money, build confidence and self-worth, and then design a plan that turns purpose into structure. She often says, *"If you're simply doing what you've always done with your mind and money, you'll be where you've always been."*

Francesca's mission in writing this book is to make a lasting impact by helping women rise into their own *Divine Wealth* by finding prosperity aligned with purpose and freedom.

Born in Leamington, Ontario, and now living in Toronto's Beach community, Francesca is a devoted mother of two who loves running, cycling, sunrise mornings, and outdoor adventures.

Learn more at www.francescarea.com.